The Rage Less Traveled

Surviving a Machete Attack

Kay Wilson

A Memoir

D1114561

OPEN WOUND PUBLISHERS

www.theragelesstraveled.com

The Rage Less Traveled

ISBN 978-1-7337522-0-6

Design & Layout: Annie Selby, Brian Thomas

www.theragelesstraveled.com

In memory of my friend Kristine Luken, and Neta Blatt-Sorek.

Written in blood and tears.

Written in gratitude for all they gave us.

Written in hope for a better world.

The Rage Less Traveled

If I were to list all the people who have held and still hold my hand to help me on my lifelong road to recovery, I sometimes feel there would not be enough paper in the world. Evil has not managed to make me cry. But the kindness that I have experienced from Jews, Muslims, Druze and Christians has made me weep. You know who you are. I am thankful to each and every one of you.

PART I

"I'm a little muddled."

—Glinda, the Good Witch of the North

CHAPTER 1

"I'm a police officer," says the woman standing beside my bed.

My heart races and blood pounds through every capillary. I need to make a run for it, to get out of here, because I am about to be sucked into a black hole. But I can't escape. Propped sitting up in a hospital bed with a tube clipped to my nostrils, wires attached to my chest, and a lung drain rammed into my left side, I can barely move.

The officer, who introduces herself as Lilach, is no older than thirty and has ebony-black hair pulled back in a ponytail and eyelashes so long they cast shadows on her cheeks. At the end of the bed, past an expanse of monitors, wires and drips, is her colleague, a bald-headed man with chubby cheeks and stubble on his chin. His name is Gil, Lilach says. They are from the Criminal Investigation Unit.

Gil sits in a plastic chair, the kind used at family barbecues on Israel's Independence Day. When he smiles, dimples like Dead Sea sinkholes open up on his cheeks.

Both dressed in jeans and leather jackets, neither looks nor acts like the police officers I'm used to – those proud-in-their-uniforms, frowning traffic cops who seem to take joy in issuing me tickets. These two are so friendly and at ease they give the impression they have just stopped by for an amiable chat. The pounding in my ears goes away, the heaviness in my arms wanes and my fingers start to tingle. I begin to feel more at ease.

3

Serene and sincere, Lilach asks if I am comfortable. I want to tell her that my side and my chest hurt like hell and my shoulder feels like it is on fire, but before I can say anything, she asks me where and when did I first meet Kristine Luken.

With the mention of that name, my eyes drag themselves away. I gaze at my sleeve. It is the clear blue of Israel's summer skies. Spoiling the beautiful color though, in smudged and patterned print, are the words "Hadassah Hospital Ein Kerem."

I allow myself to be mesmerized by colored lines that ebb and flow across the monitor screen on the other side of the bed. Beside it a sachet of yellow fluid hangs on a pole. The liquid is calm and tranquil, like a sea reflecting the golden sun. I start to feel I'm floating. Relaxed, I could be lounging on a yacht on the Mediterranean, somewhere off the coast of Tel Aviv. Nothing is going to faze me now. Dread has gone. I am ready to talk.

When I speak, my tongue dislodges a piece of dry vomit caked to the roof of my mouth. It releases an acid taste that burns my throat.

"Four months ago," I say, dabbing my lips with my sleeve. "She was part of a group I was guiding in Poland. At the end of the trip, I invited her to Israel for a long weekend."

Lilach seems surprised. "It's a long way to come for such a short time. Why would she do that?"

"Why not?" I say. "Isn't Israel worth it?"

When Lilach asks me to tell her about Kristine, the magical calm that has come over me turns into an even more wonderful sensation of brazen euphoria and unvarnished bliss. My words burst out, bubbling and toppling over each other.

"Kristine thinks everything sparkles in Israel – even the seatbelt of my old car. She's interested in stuff. I like that about her. She loves to journal and write everything down. When I was explaining about sacrifices in the Second Temple, she even underlined the word 'sacred.'"

Lilach cocks her head. "I'm a little muddled. Are you saying Kristine was – *is* – your friend as well as your client? Do you mean she was, um, *is* religious and she liked – *likes* – how you describe things in a different way? Is that what you mean?"

I can't help but grin. "Yes, that's exactly what I mean."

Lilach asks if I can tell her what happened in the Matta Forest.

"The Matta Forest? The one near Beit Shemesh? Oh, sure! Once, the whole area belonged to the tribe of Judah. Then, just a few hundred years later, the Romans, and later the Christians, and then the Muslims, all conquered the area."

I babble on, telling her that the Soreq Brook, which winds all the way from the Jerusalem Mountains to end in the Mediterranean Sea, is one of the longest drainage basins in Israel. It's also famous for a curious and surprising Israelite victory that involved hemorrhoids and the Ark of the Covenant. Does she know the story? Maybe Officer Gil knows the story?

Officer Gil stares at his lap.

I do not want, on any account, to tell her about what happened in the Matta Forest, or even to think about it. So instead I tell her how Kristine and I hunted for ancient pottery at Tel Beit Shemesh, an ancient Israelite city snuggled between the foothills that protected Jerusalem.

"We found some broken jug handles. Coarse, thick and brick red, typical Iron Age. They're plentiful around there. They weren't worth anything, honestly they weren't. We only took a few, unlike this family we saw there. They were looters. They had even brought buckets with them."

The policewoman doesn't seem bothered by their, or our, helping ourselves to broken antiquities. She looks at me and says there are more worthless pieces of chipped pottery in Israel than there are grains of sand.

"Did you meet anyone else there?" she asks.

"Eyal Golan."

She raises her eyebrows. "Eyal Golan?"

"His music was blasting out of a huge, shiny jeep, the kind rich husbands buy their bored wives just to go shopping. It was sprawled under a tree and pilfered the only shade. People can be so thoughtless. Anyway, I told Kristine to bring her notebook because I was going to teach her how to identify ancient pottery. I also told her that Eyal Golan is the Israeli version of Julio Iglesias. She loves to write everything down, but I told her she didn't need to write down the bit about Eyal Golan."

Lilach looks at me as if I'm an orphaned kitten.

I carry on. "After that we went to visit the Sea Horse Winery in Moshav Bar Giora."

Her colleague jolts up. "Did you drink?"

What nerve! The man has said nothing until now and suddenly all he wants to know is, did I drink. Who does he think I am? I might like my wine, but I'm not stupid enough to drink and drive and swerve the car all over the State of Israel.

Lilach throws him a frown. As if on cue, he gives me his best smile. I scowl at him, hoping he feels bad for even thinking I may have been drunk.

I tell them that Kristine said the moshav looked like a Swiss village and she loved everything about it, even the sign on the doors of the winery. "Do you know it? It's the logo of the Ministry of Tourism: Joshua ben Nun and Caleb clutching a cluster of grapes returning from their espionage mission in the Promised Land. I told Kristine the grapes are far too big for the people who live in the little houses of Moshav Bar Giora. She laughed and wrote that down."

Lilach looks at her watch. "Who did you meet there, Kay?"

"Only the winemaker. Nice chap. Because Kristine doesn't speak Hebrew, he gave us a private tour in English. We tried a wine called 'Lennon.' It's named after John. Extremely tasty. I didn't try 'The Wright Brothers' or 'Ernest Hemingway' though, because I was driving. Kristine bought a few bottles for her parents and told me Joshua ben Nun would have been proud of her. She even bought me a bottle as well. We'll try some when I get home."

The policewoman again prompts me to tell her about the Matta Forest. She knows it's hard for me, but it's really very important. Could I do that for her please?

I shrug, and it feels as if someone is walloping me on the shoulder with a brick. I clutch the rail of the bed and wait for the pain to subside.

"What time did you get there, Kay?"

My voice is flat. "About three, although we nearly didn't get there at all. I almost missed the turn to the entrance, because the sign to Horvat Hanut is hidden behind some trees. Anyway, I saw it just in time. We started off with the mosaic. Do you know it? It's the remains of a

Byzantine church. About a thousand years ago, the Muslims built an inn over it. Kristine asked who destroyed the church floor. I can't remember exactly what I said. Anyway, after that we … we … we went for a walk."

When I say "walk," Peanut, my sweet little Jack Russell-Pinscher mix, pops into my mind. How I wish she were lying on my chest right now, nudging her nose into my neck. Starting with the tips of her ears, I would roll them down and squeeze them into her ear holes, before unfolding them again. She loves that. When she has enough, she likes to roll over onto her back so I can tickle her tummy. If I stop too soon, she twists her head and prods me with her nose, to make me do it again.

"I want my dog," I whimper. "I want Peanut."

Lilach takes my hand. "Your dog is with the paramedic, Kay. He went back to the forest to find her. She really is OK. She has a small wound on her leg which he stitched up." She lets go of my hand and holds her thumb and finger an inch apart, to show me how small Peanut's injury is.

I am intrigued by a baffling and peculiar sound of water being sucked down a drain. Stranger still, the noise is coming from me. I lift the sheet to peek. The gurgling is coming from the lung drain, the inch-wide tube inserted into my left side. Ruby rivulets are bubbling through it into a plastic container on the floor.

Those are my insides! My insides are dripping into that box on the floor!

The monitor is doing strange things too. Normally a regular beat, the tempo is off and unpredictable. The colored lines that only moments ago were moving across the screen like rolling waves, are frantic, zany and jagged.

Lilach leans close to my face. "Kay, try to relax," she says, glancing at the monitor. "No one will hurt you. I need to know what happened in the forest and I really need to know now."

I look up at the window. The sky is velvet black. Come up to the sky, Kay, my brain says. Come up. So I float up until I am looking down on me. There I am, sitting up in bed, dressed in oversized, sky-blue pajamas talking to a courteous woman in casual clothing who says she is a policewoman.

The Rage Less Traveled

I listen to myself speak as if I'm listening to my own voice on a radio. I am neither here, nor there; I am somewhere in-between. In a voice so calm it is chilling, I hear myself tell the policewoman,

"They wanted water."

"Find yourself a place where you won't get into any trouble."

—Aunty Em

CHAPTER 2

Hidden behind a clump of trees on a serpentine road southeast of Beit Shemesh is a rusty road sign that marks the entrance to Horvat Hanut. It catches drivers by surprise, causing them to speed by for a couple of miles before they can turn around. Although I know the sign is there, I am distracted by the music coming from the car speakers: Oscar Peterson's jazz piano arrangement of the classic "Somewhere Over the Rainbow." Only at the very last second do I see the sign, slam on the brakes and skid into the unpaved carpark at the entrance of the Israel National Trail, right in the heart of the Matta Forest.

Ashen-faced and wide-eyed in the passenger seat, Kristine Luken clutches Peanut and presses imaginary brakes with her feet.

I apologize for being preoccupied, but tell her she should know that two sons of cantors wrote "Somewhere Over the Rainbow" on the eve of World War Two. Kristine says she had no idea that the music from *The Wizard of Oz* had anything to do with Jews, or that the song might also be about a Jewish hope for a better world.

Her fascination with Jewish history, her questions and her respect for other people's traditions birthed a fast friendship, albeit an unexpected one. We are completely different. She is an American who moved to England. Born in Britain, I moved to Israel. She is Christian and I am Jewish. Kristine looks younger than her forty-four years. Unlike me, she likes to go to the gym, eat vegan, wear make-up, fan her long wavy brown hair and iron her clothes. Her cream hiking pants and black fleece jacket are without a crease. When I told her this morning that many Israelis never use an iron, her mouth dropped open.

Kristine is well-mannered. She prefaces every sentence with "please" and ends with "thank you," a habit that I have largely dropped since moving here in the '80's to live under Israel's burning sun alongside my scorched, and sometimes impatient, countrymen.

I check my backpack. I have everything we need for the hour-long hike: map, phone, purse, water, apples, my penknife for peeling, a packet of sunflower seeds for an extra snack, and some *baklava*, a Middle Eastern pastry stuffed with chopped nuts glued together with honey. The *baklava* was given to me by Khalil Nazari, my good-humored colleague, an Israeli Arab tour bus driver I work with when guiding groups around Israel. True to form, Khalil has roguishly attached an "invoice" to the *baklava* to suggest I "owe him" for the gift. I love that man. If I had a dollar for every time he and his wife spoiled me with their cultural delicacies, I could build myself a palace overlooking Jerusalem.

Kristine wonders aloud if she should take her notebook. It's the same one she was using in the summer when we met in Poland. I was one of three tour guides leading a group of Christians on a ten-day historical tour of Holocaust sites, in what during the Second World War was Nazi-occupied Poland. It was my first time there, which made me the rookie. I was there as much to learn about Jewish life before the Holocaust as I was to guide about the death of it. One of the keenest students in the group, Kristine had been so busy taking notes about Jews and Nazis that she barely looked out of the bus window.

She decides to leave her notebook in the car. Should she take her passport though? Of course she should, she mutters to herself, she should take any other valuables too.

She hands me an envelope. Inside are one hundred British pounds, the notes so crisp they could have been starched. When I tell her we had agreed to settle up later for the guiding fee, she just shrugs.

Peanut can't wait any longer. She leaps out of the car window and bounds toward the picnic area, where under the shade of the pine trees, families while away the lazy Sabbath afternoon. Men poke slabs of meat on grills, children play ball and women arrange tubs of Israeli salad on picnic tables. The Matta Forest is an oasis of peace in what is sometimes a dry and unforgiving land.

Behind a clump of olive trees are the ruins of Horvat Hanut, a thousand-year-old Islamic inn built over a destroyed Byzantine church that sat on the ancient road between Jerusalem and the port of Gaza. I plan to show Kristine the mosaic church floor before we begin our hike. Almost intact, it is one of the least known in Israel and also one of the prettiest.

We walk over to the mosaic, dodging a little boy on a buggy. Tied to the steering wheel are blue and white balloons with "Happy Birthday" printed on them in Hebrew. Peddling furiously, the little fellow swerves around Peanut, squealing, "Move puppy, move!"

To allow the public to enjoy the antiquities, the Jewish National Fund leaves tatty old brooms at the entrance. These are so people can sweep away the sand that protects the mosaic from the elements. They are expected to cover it up again with sand before they leave.

I hand Kristine a broom, but she is too excited. Falling to her knees, she sweeps away the sand with her bare hands. Puffs of yellow waft into the air. Her green-blue eyes are filled with wonder, as if she is opening a treasure chest. Soon the first mosaic squares appear, richly colored chestnut, claret and ruby, spelling out an inscription in Greek. The letters are framed with images of vines, pomegranates and what looks like a sacrificed sheep. Placed together with such precision, the mosaic pieces look like pixels.

Part of the mosaic is damaged. In antiquity, Christians of all denominations decorated their holy places. However, faces and animals were not only frowned upon by some denominations, but also by Muslims. These groups perceived the representations as "graven images," and therefore sacrilege.

"This destruction of art in the name of religion is called iconoclasm," I tell Kristine, refraining from saying I think it's intolerance.

I pull her to her feet. It's three o'clock. Time to hike.

I pick up a couple of pinecones and hurl them ahead. Peanut scampers after them, ears flattened against her head, then bounds back to me, empty-mouthed, begging me to do it again. This is my favorite of all her various ear positions; with her ears glued to her head, she seems more vulnerable and sweeter than ever.

A wooden sign marks the start of the Caesar's Path. Once a Roman road, the path has been incorporated into the extraordinary 600-mile Israel National Trail, which wends its way from Kibbutz Dan in the north through varied and breathtaking landscapes down to Eilat, the southernmost point of Israel, on the Red Sea. This trail is iconic in Israeli culture. Thousands, young and old, hike along it, sometimes over many months, sometimes in one long trek.

We walk in silence, enjoying the tranquility of the forest. Sometimes the intermittent sound of cars traveling along the Elah Valley below seeps through. Today, Renaults, Suzukis and Mazdas drive along the valley where Roman chariots once stormed.

Like most other days since I have lived in Israel, the afternoon of December 18, 2010, is bright and clear. Having spent my childhood under England's slate-gray skies, I have never grown tired of Israel's warm light. The sun streams down between the trees, dousing the shrubs and bushes in an orange hue. Lining the trail are the trees that typically make for a Mediterranean woodland: terebinths, holly oaks, and the distinct rubbery-leaved carobs. The evergreen pines and the wild olive trees with their musty leaves seem unfazed that there has been no rain so far, but when the cloudbursts finally begin, it will take only days before purple, pink and white cyclamens begin to dot around the bases of these trees. It is especially on days such as today, with a perfect sky, perfect nature, and perfect little birds chirping in the trees, that I breathe an extra sigh of contentment for having moved to Israel nearly three decades ago.

Not that England was bad; it was just that the world was too tempting and too interesting for me to shut myself away in an office in London gazing at rain slashing against the windowpane. Israel gave me purpose. I wanted to live here, to be part of my people and my land, and contribute to its growth. It's not all rosy here, though. Sometimes Israel and I do not see eye to eye. This strikes me when people are late for an appointment, or push in line, or expect me to use one of those non-absorbent, waxy, ineffective napkins that come with *falafel*, or when men stop anywhere on the side of the road, at any time of day or night, to take a pee.

But I love Israel because Israel deserves to be loved: the vitality of the people, the optimism despite the hardships, the lack of social pecking orders and the willingness to help and welcome strangers. There is a lot to show off about Israel and much to boast about. The incredible medical, agricultural, technical and cultural Jewish contributions make for a thriving state. I wish more tourists would come here for the same reasons that they venture to any other country, because it is interesting, or because it is a fine place to explore, to meet the people, or just to have a good time.

Kristine stops beside a carob tree and cranes her neck to look at the generous canopy. In ancient times, carob seeds were used as a unit of mass, because every seed weighs exactly the same. Every tree has significance in Jewish culture. Olive branches famously represent peace, the palm is a symbol for victory, and the carob represents justice, because the seeds are equal in weight. Kristine is entranced: Whether she is hearing about the composers of "Somewhere Over the Rainbow," the damaged mosaic, the olives of peace, the palms of victory, or the carobs of justice, for her, this is the Holy Land in every sense, where even a seed is sacred.

As we walk, she recalls our lunchtime visit at the Sea Horse Winery in Moshav Bar Giora. Did I see how the winemaker held his glass up to the light? Did I see he had purple stains on his fingers? She tells me she loved it when he swished the wine in his glass in circles, and she copied him. She didn't know it was to let in the oxygen. Why didn't I tell her that? She asks me if I thought it was funny when she asked him if Jesus drank wine, and he joked that Jesus wasn't a Baptist. She will never forget how to pronounce "L'chayim," "To life," the Hebrew way. The best bit, she thinks, was when we all clinked our glasses together. She loves how Jewish people drink to life.

We come to a barren, dry patch at the side of the trail. It is surrounded by a wire fence that protects four freshly dug holes that await the planting of saplings. Stooping under the wire, Kristine tiptoes over to the piles of the russet earth and bends down to touch the soil, which is known as "rendzina," apparently after a Polish word meaning "to chatter," because the gravel in the soil pings and clicks on the plough as if it is chattering to the farmer.

While she examines the saplings, I mull over our itinerary. After Kristine arrived late last night, this is the first day of her four-day trip. Today we're exploring the Judaean Mountains; tomorrow, Sunday, is the first day of the week and everything will be open again. We will take in Jerusalem: the City of David, the Temple Mount and the excavations at the Southern Wall. She is very fit so we will walk the ramparts of the Old City too. On Monday, we'll head south and go for a dip in the Dead Sea, climb Masada and hike in the desert oasis of Ein Gedi. On her last day, we'll drive north to the Galilee. She'll love it there.

As the path meanders westwards through the trees, I tell her a little more about myself.

"After moving to Israel, it took a couple of decades before I knew what I really wanted to do. At first, I didn't really care. It was as if being in Israel was enough. I was part of something bigger than me, I was part of our history, working to maximize the present for the sake of our future."

That's how I felt. I tried everything from working inside sun-struck hothouses plucking bell peppers in gloves three sizes too big for me, to doodling portraits on the streets to sell to passersby, to running an arts and crafts shop in Jaffa's flea market, to playing piano in smoky bars that sold cheap scotch. I loved it all: the grit under my nails, the pokey taverns of Tel Aviv, the buzz of the flea market, and the satisfaction of handing someone a cartoon of themselves that they actually liked.

When I say I love guiding the most, Kristine smiles in approval.

"Guiding is a pleasure," I say. "When I look at my watch, it's not to wish the hours away, but only to check if I'm running to schedule."

Kristine looks awestruck. So I joke around, mocking the way Israelis are able to contend with wars, conflicts and the threat of Iran, but the country implodes whenever it rains.

Nothing bursts her bubble. She thinks Israelis are amazing, which secretly makes me feel rather proud.

Ahead, the trail squeezes through the forest and out of sight. To our left are ancient limestone steps that lead down to a Roman water cistern and will take us in a circle back to the carpark. To the right and uphill, five minutes' walk away, is the only lookout on the trail. From there, I can show her Tel Beit Shemesh, where this morning we searched for ancient pottery. I have never seen anyone treat shards the way Kristine does. Every time she found one, she placed it on her fleece jacket as carefully as if she were laying a baby down to sleep.

When I ask her now if she wants to go up to the lookout so we can see Tel Beit Shemesh, she sets a condition: If we bump into the same family we saw this morning, this time I have to be nice.

I can't resist teasing her. "You mean the rustlers who expropriated my shade, or do you mean that mother, father and those two sulky teenagers who brought buckets and spades, as if they were going to the beach for the day? It looked like they were going to loot every single shard there."

Kristine disagrees. She thinks it was special to see a family of amateur archaeologists digging up their history. That's Kristine. She loves to see the good in people.

I glance at my watch. We have been walking for thirty minutes. It will take us about the same amount of time to return to the car. Not only is there enough time to head up to the lookout, from which I can show her why Beit Shemesh was such a strategic Biblical town, but later we'll also be able to catch the sun set over Kibbutz Netiv HaLamed Heh. Situated a stone's throw from where David fought Goliath, the kibbutz is named after a group of thirty-five young Jewish fighters who were notoriously massacred and mutilated by the Arab enemy during Israel's War of Independence. I won't tell Kristine that; she hates violence.

Fleece jacket now tied around her waist, she follows me uphill through the thicket towards the lookout. Like me, Kristine is unfazed by the thorns and spiked purple thistles that are part of every Israeli forest.

After a few minutes, we reach the brow of the hill. The pines and cypress thin out like curtains drawing aside. The view in front of us is unobstructed.

The dry riverbed of the Zanoah Brook flaunts its beauty. Its southern flanks swoop down to end in the chalky, seductive purple valley. In the winter, dry riverbeds such as these can flood without warning. Torrents of rain run off the hillsides, causing flash floods to catch hikers by surprise and sweep them off their feet. In the desert, flash floods can even sweep cars off the road.

On the slopes to the west are the white high-rise apartments of the new suburb Ramat Beit Shemesh. The balconies jut out, casting black shadows on the bleached walls beneath them. Kristine thinks they look like giant piano keys.

Away to the northeast, peeking out behind the cypress trees, are the smoked-chili-red roofs of Moshav Bar Giora. I lick my lips, still able to taste the Cabernet Sauvignon from our wine-tasting visit. The vineyards that line both sides of the village are barren and look dead. But they aren't: Come August, they will be pregnant with grapes once more. Kristine tells me how she loved the checkered curtains and pots of pink and orange geraniums on the windowsills. She thinks the moshav looked like Switzerland, not a farming community in the Middle East. If she listens carefully, I tell her, she may still be able to hear the free-range chickens clucking as they strut down the narrow, graveled road.

Directly east, the Judaean Mountains bulge like biceps protecting Jerusalem. In Biblical times, Abraham, Isaac and Jacob lived and moved along the ridge of these heights, traveling back and forth from Beersheba, up through Hebron, Bethlehem, Bethel and Shiloh. Today these places lie beyond the Green Line. They have been under the jurisdiction of the Palestinian Authority since 1993.

Kristine asks if we can go there.

"When we get back home we can Google it," I say. "Don't worry, you're not missing out. We have so much to see and enjoy on our side of things."

We decide to sit down, rest for a few minutes and enjoy the view. Under the shade of a nearby carob tree is a slab of limestone. Even in the heat of the day, Jerusalem's mountainous rock feels cool. We watch a couple of grasshoppers take refuge in the shade of a stone. Ants scissor a leaf apart with their strong little jaws, then drag the pieces to their comrades a couple of feet away. The forest is like an orchestra. Crickets click like castanets, a warbler lets loose a soprano vibrato, doves coo like pan flutes, flies hum like the roll on a snare and Kristine gazes across at the Zanoah Brook, humming, "Somewhere Over the Rainbow."

It's time to teach her how to eat sunflower seeds the Israeli way. I open my backpack and take out a handful of seeds, explaining that the trick is to crack the shell with her teeth and release the seed into her mouth, then spit out the shell, all without using her hands.

I put a seed between my teeth and spit it out with a Bronx cheer. With cheeks red and eyes watering, Kristine laughs as if this is the funniest thing she has ever seen. I like making people laugh, and she is an easy target for that. She has found many things we have seen today funny, especially my landlord, Mr. Gershoni, an elderly, slightly deaf, former New Yorker. We spotted him this morning as we were about to set off from my home in Givat Ze'ev. He saw us in the car and beelined towards Kristine and pressed his face against the passenger window. The veins bulged on his neck. "With eyes like that, there's not a man in the Middle East who wouldn't want you as his lady," the old flirt said.

The Rage Less Traveled

I take another seed and aim to spit the shell as far as I can. Sixty feet down the slope of the hill, something catches my eye.

Two men are crouching in the bushes.

"It's a twister, it's a twister!"

—Hunk, the farm hand

CHAPTER 3

I signal Kristine to keep quiet. Peanut, oblivious, sniffs her way down the slope of the hill towards them. Dumb dog! If she gets any closer, they'll know we're here. Suddenly, Peanut stops. Body rigid, she growls.

The bushes rustle. The men stand up. "Have you got any water?" one calls out in Arab-accented Hebrew.

"I wish," I say back in Hebrew, trying to sound nonchalant. They turn around and disappear back through the thicket and out of sight.

Kristine asks what they wanted.

"Only water," I say, in a tight voice. "They only wanted water."

My heart is pounding and I am far from calm. What on earth were they doing hiding in the bushes? Were they spying on us? What if they saw my backpack? All our valuables are in it.

I pull Kristine to her feet and tell her that we should get back to the car. There are plenty of other things we still need to see.

She starts to scoop up the crumbs from our picnic.

"Leave it," I snap.

With Kristine following me, we hurry back downhill in the direction of the car. Loose stones under our feet threaten to trip us. It is very thorny too. Without stopping, I grope in the side pouch of my backpack for my penknife. We will be in a mess if they steal my bag. It holds my car keys, my wallet, my money, my ID and Kristine's passport. Not wanting to alarm her, I hide the knife in my right hand.

Back to her happy self, Peanut whizzes by, snapping at flies. I feel swells of relief. The men must have gone. They really must have only wanted water. How stupid of me. I should have taken the time to find the easiest way back to the trail. We will just have to keep going, at least we'll be back on it soon.

I begin to think about what to do for the rest of the day. It's only a quarter to four, way too early to make our way to the sunset view. I promised Kristine that we would pop in sometime to my neighbors, Rabbi and Mrs. Feinberg. Personally, I would rather go to a wine bar or jazz club than talk religion all night, but Kristine so enjoyed chatting to them as we waited at the stoplight in Giv'at Ze'ev. I could see it in her eyes. When we pulled away, she told me in an awestruck voice that she had never spoken to a rabbi before. She was surprised that his skullcap was embroidered with "Beit Shemesh Blue Sox," the name of a local baseball team, and not with a Bible verse. I'll call them and say we'll be coming. That's what we'll do. They love having people over. It will be—

Kristine screams.

What feels like a log rams into my back, blasting air out of my lungs. I am knocked face first to the ground. My lip splits open. Dirt shoots up my nose. Someone is rubbing my face in the ground. I can't breathe. I kick and struggle and somehow manage to wiggle onto my back.

The man locks his hands around my wrists and presses his face against mine. His bristles scour my skin. I toss my head from side to side to avoid his rancid breath. He knees his way up my torso, gouging the air from my chest. I twist my wrists and manage to free my left hand, enabling me to thump him on his chin. He lets go of me and jerks back. Seeing my chance, I stab him between his legs. Metal glides into flesh. Blood spurts onto my sleeve. He covers his crotch with his hand.

"*Koos emek*," he curses in Arabic, grabbing my wrist and shaking it until the knife drops. He takes me by the scruff of my neck and hauls me to my feet. Then, he slides his hand under his jacket and draws out a serrated knife, almost a foot long.

Urine trickles down my thighs. The ground seesaws under me. My knees quiver and all I can do is try not to vomit. He barks at me to sit.

Kristine! Where is Kristine?

She is ten feet away, being held by another man who has one arm wrapped around her neck, forcing her head up. In his other hand, he holds a long, curved kitchen knife to her throat. Her chin is juddering against his sleeve.

In utter shock, all I can do is gape at the men. Incongruous, the one who attacked me is wearing an Israeli police jacket. His rat-like ears are set low on the side of his wide-browed head and his open mouth reveals uneven, yellow teeth. The other man is also hideous: squashed nose, thick lips, and black wiry eyebrows joined in the middle. Both have empty, lifeless eyes.

Kristine's assailant shoves her so hard she trips.

"Here!" I say, patting the ground in a frenzy. "Come here!"

She scurries towards me on her hands and knees. Her lips are gray and her face is marble-white with streaks of pink.

We sit side by side, hugging our knees, with Kristine's assailant hovering over us with legs astride and his hands on his hips. The other one slouches against a tree. Like a grizzly bear, he rubs his back against the trunk. Itch satisfied, he fumbles in his top pocket and takes out a packet of cigarettes. He lights one and tosses the packet to his partner. With a machete in one hand and a Marlboro in the other, for them it seems to be just another working day.

Over the oblivious twittering birds, I strain to hear for the sounds of possible hikers below on the National Trail. We are not more than three hundred feet from the path. We are so near help, yet so far away.

The sun beats down and time stands still. Sweat drips into my eyes. My tongue is so rough and dry it feels as if it's covered in sandpaper. The raging and obsessive thirst has paralyzed my ability to think of anything except for the thought that this can't be happening to me. My clothes stick to my skin. I want to take off my jacket, but I don't dare. They'll think I'm trying something. They'll panic and knife me. I must leave it on and sweat it out.

Suddenly, I see Peanut in the bushes. Ears down, she comes out and edges towards me. The attacker dressed as a policeman lunges towards her. She yelps and scampers away.

Failing to grab the dog, he picks up my backpack strewn on the ground and takes out my water bottle. When he holds it up, the sun reflects on the water, making it look so luscious. Even a drop would help bring me to my senses.

"Please," I rasp, in English. "Just a sip."

Ignoring me, he glugs until it is all gone and tosses the bottle to the ground. He strides over to join his partner and snaps his fingers at us to stand. The men face us, scrutinizing us.

The "policeman" eyes my hips and inches nearer. I stiffen my legs, clench my pelvis and wait for the worst. He slides his hand into the side pocket of my pants and pulls out my cell phone.

"Switch it off," he barks in Hebrew, slamming it into my hand.

My whole arm shakes. I am so clumsy that I can only press random buttons that make absurd little happy key tones ring out in the forest. He grabs the phone, fiddles with it, successfully turns it off, and stuffs it into his pocket. Next, he takes out Kristine's passport from my backpack.

Her voice is shattering. "I'm an American citizen. Take it, have it!"

Hearing her brings me to my senses. "We're both tourists," I say in English. "Really we are."

With a sneer, he hands the passport to his partner, then delves again into my bag. This time he takes out my wallet. Eyes wide, he pulls out the money, stuffs it into his pocket and continues his search.

The blood drains from my face. He has found my Israeli identity card. If he can read Hebrew, he will see the word "Jew." Frantically, I try to think of something to distract him. I don't need to. He pulls out my car keys.

"Where is it?" he asks in Hebrew.

No longer able to play the game of tourist, I answer him in Hebrew.

"At the mosaic," I say.

"What kind?"

I stretch my arms, and the truth, to exaggerate the size of my little Nissan Micra. If they think my car is big and expensive, they may leave us alone and just bolt with the vehicle. He nods to his partner. They move away a few feet and whisper among themselves.

I take the chance to speak to Kristine. In a low voice, I speak as fast as I can.

"They're going to let us go. They're just a couple of thieves. They want the car, that's all. Whatever you do, don't panic. We'll soon be free. As soon as we get out of here, we'll go to the police. Remember what they look like."

Color floods back to her cheeks and lips. As our lives slip out of danger, relief replaces confusion. It's only a robbery. Thank God, it's only a robbery!

Under the pines, delirium comes. In this place, *"where happy little bluebirds fly,"* we will soon skip through the forest, climb every hillock, smell every flower and kiss every tree. We will soon be free!

I try to take in every detail. Both mid-thirties. Around six feet tall. Israeli army pants and Israeli police jacket, too short at the sleeves. Light gray jeans and dirty short all-weather jacket. Crooked teeth. Unibrow.

They stop talking and come towards us. One rips my guide badge off from around my neck then grabs my arm, the other seizes Kristine. They hustle us uphill farther away from the National Trail, towards a less exposed area. The pine trees cage us in. Over the sound of our trudging feet, I hear Kristine whimper, Jesus, help me, Jesus, please help me.

They yank us to a halt and order us not to move. Once again, they step away to whisper between themselves. Kristine is bone-white and blue-lipped. Strands of hair are plastered to her forehead. Her trembling gives me an idea.

"Quick! Fake an epileptic fit. A medical crisis will make them panic and let us go."

She starts to convulse. It's not enough.

"Harder!" I hiss. "Fucking harder."

Beads of sweat fly off her brow. I can see the whites of her eyes.

In a choked voice, I call out to the men. "She's sick. Her medicine is in the car. Her illness makes her scream."

Imploring them with my eyes, I wait for them to see sense. When they stomp towards us, waving their knives, Kristine shakes harder than ever.

Until now, not panicking had been crucial. Now, completely trapped, the only choice I have is to choose what kind of panic will cause us the least harm. If we scream to alert possible hikers on the trail, I don't know if we will even be heard. Even if someone does hear us, these thugs will knife us before help arrives. If we make a run for it, we won't get far. They're big men and can easily outrun us. Out of options, ideas and even the ability to string together any more thoughts, I gamble on the last and what seems to be the least severe option: to stay where we are and obey.

The "policeman" hovers beside us while the other moves aside a few feet to make a phone call. As he mumbles into the phone, he twists his knife and watches the sun glint off the blade.

In less than a minute, he's back. They speak to each other again. By the nodding of heads, it seems they have a plan.

The "policeman" steps towards me. "Take off your shoes!"

My hands are trembling now with rage. How obscene, threatening us with knives and leaving us to walk barefoot through the thorns.

"Take out the laces."

I want to slap his fucking face.

"Hands behind your back."

He grabs my wrists. As he ties them with the laces, I try to leave a small gap between them so I will have room later to wiggle free. While he binds up Kristine, I grind my wrists up and down and side to side. With each attempt, the laces cut my skin. He has tied them tighter than I thought.

Suddenly, his face is inches away from mine. He curses me again, for trying to get free. A thread of spit hangs from his mouth. He reties the laces, this time grunting and yanking. My fingers throb. He must have cut off the circulation. My hands must be black and blue.

The other man tugs Kristine's fleece jacket off from around her waist. He holds it up and slashes it with his knife, then rips it apart with his hands.

"Please don't kill us," I cry. "Please."

"We good," says my attacker in English. He puts his hand on his heart. "We won't kill you," he reassures me in Hebrew. As if offended that I could think so badly of him, he pouts.

He gags me with a strip of her torn fleece, while the other one gags Kristine. I suck on the material. Hot, stale air seeps through.

The "policeman" takes off my sunglasses, strapped around my neck. Next, he tinkers with the clasp of my Star of David necklace. Breathing heavily, his mouth hangs open revealing his uneven yellow teeth wedged into patchy, salmon gums. Necklace successfully undone, he tucks the pendant into his pocket.

Shoeless, bound and gagged, Kristine and I stand side by side. Her assailant moves away a few feet to make another phone call. This time I can hear what is being said. Even though my Arabic is limited, I can understand that he is asking about "a driver."

As the sun begins to set, a realization dawns: We are going to be kidnapped.

Instead of being shoved down the hill into a waiting car, I am pushed to my knees. A piece of fleece is placed over my head. It covers only my left eye. Out of the corner of my right, I suddenly see a light; the sun glinting off his machete.

I no longer hear the birds, or the crickets, or the rustle of the leaves. I hear only my heartbeat. Numb to fear and emptied of feeling, I kneel motionless and wait for him to hack off my head,

"*Allahu Akbar!*"

"Jesus!"

"*Shema Yisrael!*" He stabs me in the back with such force it knocks me to the ground. I am lying on my right side, with him kneeling on my left thigh. My bones crunch and my flesh rips. I am on fire. Every time he plunges his foot-long knife into my side and back, it causes a pain so searing that everything goes momentarily white. Sometimes the serrated steel wedges into bone and he has to tug to get it out. At other times, the knife slides easily into and out of flesh and organs.

I can't take it in. I'm forty-six years old. I'm too young to die. Murder is something that happens to other people. It can't be happening to me!

The seconds between each stab are as much of a torment as the knife itself. He isn't in a hurry. Each blow is harder, deeper, wider, and more excruciating than the previous one. Please God, if only he would stab me in a different place.

Kristine is six feet away lying on her back. With her hands tied behind her, she has nothing but her shoulders to try to fend off his knife. Groaning and whimpering, she writhes and squirms. Grunting and heaving, he hacks and cleaves. Oh God, Jesus, she gurgles over the songs of the little birds.

My only chance is to play dead. I keep my eyes open because I think it is more convincing. And in doing so, I watch her die to save my life.

Then, they are gone.

Peanut lets out a yelp. They must have killed her too. Unable to care, I just lie there. The ground begins to vibrate. Footsteps. They're coming back!

I am rolled onto my back. The orange, purple and red sky is suddenly obscured by a silhouette of jagged steel. He thrusts the blade into my chest, where my Star of David had been. I don't blink, flinch or move.

"I've been dying to tell you what I thought of you."

—Aunty Em

CHAPTER 4

Over what sounds like soup bubbling, birds twitter and flies hum. It is a bewitching noise that woos me to close my eyes. Eternal sleep, kind and tender, is beckoning me. Warm and at peace, my mind drifts, thinking pleasantly how, once-upon-a-world-ago, I went for a walk in a beautiful forest. That was then. And then is gone.

While thinking this, I gaze lazily at a soggy mass of maroon in the bushes.

Kristine. That's Kristine!

I too will soon be dead. I have to get up and make it to a place where someone will find my body. I owe that much to Kristine. I owe it to her family. I owe it to my family, and to all the people I love, and I owe it to myself. If I stay here and fall asleep, it will be forever.

With hands tied behind my back, I can't balance or push myself up, so I dig the side of my heel into the ground and lever myself up with my elbow and the side of my leg. I manage to twist myself up into a kneeling position. When I shake my head to move the flies gorging on the blood on my face, my body topples forward. My face lands between two rocks. Frenzied white dots dance behind my eyes.

God, please. I don't have long. I can't die here. I *have* to get up.

Using my forehead as a lever, I push my head back from the rock until I am kneeling again. Unable to sustain its own weight, my head hangs. I catch sight of a piece of bone poking out of my blooded side. Tangy spew hurtles up my throat. I hastily swallow.

With my last strength, I manage to stand. I eye the abyss of the Zanoah Brook below. My wrists throb so hard that my fingers feel like they are about to explode. My torso is so heavy my knees could be supporting an oak tree. I try to steady myself, making sure not to look across at the maroon in the bushes. If I see what's left of Kristine, I will die in a heap beside her.

The worst is over. In minutes from now, there will be no more pain ever again. All I need to do is to take it one step at a time. That is what I must do, take it one step at a time. The journey will be thorny, for the most uphill and unmarked, but I have to try. Someone has to find my body.

Turning my back on Kristine's death, I take the first step towards my own.

Cold rips through my bones. It's like being inside a fridge. There is so little air, I could be breathing through a straw. Thistles rip my ankles, thorns pierce my feet. With my tongue I to try to loosen the bits of acidic vomit caked to the roof of my mouth and open up a bigger airway.

Faces of the people I love appear in the gnarled tree trunks. They are contorted with grief. The branches become their arms and claw at my clothes. They are holding me back from my grave. To think that I will never see them again, or hug them, or tell them that I love them, sends shudders through my body. It's too late to say the things I never had the courage to say. Never again will I hear the howl of the wind, or laughter, or music, or see the endless ocean and the desert massifs. My home, my land, my life and those that I love, have come to an end.

Tears choke me. The grief, the loss and the consuming anguish bring me to a standstill. But I can't give up here. I have to get to a place where someone will find my body. I need to think of something else.

I imagine a piano.

Notes weave around each other and form "Somewhere Over the Rainbow." With each step, I imagine a chord, and with each chord I edge one step closer to the world to come.

As I toy between a D flat and G flat major, through the trees down the hill, about five hundred feet away, I suddenly spot the serpentine road. The road that leads to Horvat Hanut! I've made it. It's good enough. I don't even have to find the trail. I must choose my place of death with care, though. There is no sidewalk along that road. Cars speed around the corners and always see things too late. If it looks like a road accident, Kristine may never be found.

A few feet ahead are some low flat rocks. I edge towards them. They provide relief from the thorns. When I step down and back into the thicket, something soft brushes my ankles.

Peanut.

Through eyes blurred with tears, I look down at my little dog. Her leg is bloody, her ears are down.

Stay with me, Peanut. Die with me, Peanut.

With blood and time running out, five hundred feet could be five hundred miles. The road is not getting closer and I'm getting weaker with every step. I am dizzy. It feels like I am at high altitude. I can't go on. Right here will do. I look down to search for the most comfortable spot to die. When I kick away some twigs to prepare the ground for my burial, the sandy soil balms the gashes on my feet.

Sandy soil?

It's the trail! The National Trail! I have reached the National Trail!

Suddenly, I hear voices.

I look up. Fifty feet ahead are a group of people walking towards an open-backed truck parked in a clearing. If I can get their attention, someone will see me before I die.

I try to speed up. I rub my chin against my chest, trying to shift the gag. Look this way, damn you! Look at me!

Things happen in slow motion: A man points his key remote towards the truck. The people open the doors. They get in. They close the doors. Then the truck drives away, leaving a billow of dust and tire marks in the dirt.

I don't care, I can't anymore. All that is left is to declare the eternal creed of *Shema Yisrael* and beg Heaven for mercy. Blinking away the tears, I begin to pray in Hebrew, my last words ever.

Hear, O Israel, the Lord is our God, the Lord—

Wait. That's giggling. I can hear giggling.

I look up. About seventy feet away a group of children are playing ball beside a clump of trees. Next to them are a couple of women sitting at a picnic table and two men barbecuing in a haze of smoke.

Morbidly euphoric that I have been given this one last chance to speak to someone before I die, I muster new strength and begin to count the final steps that will lead me to my death.

One, two, three …

Aware that the sight of me could cause the children life-long trauma, I veer left so the adults will be between me and them.

Fourteen, fifteen, sixteen …

To get the attention of the women at the table, I scuff my feet. A cloud of dirt rises. Oblivious, they stuff paper plates into plastic bags. They still don't look up. For God's sake, look up. I can't go on!

Twenty-eight, twenty-nine …

Behind me, the low sun casts my shadow long and black. As I draw closer, it spreads like spilt ink over the picnic table. A woman looks up. Her shriek sends shivers through the forest.

"The sooner you get out of Oz, the safer you'll sleep, my dear."

—Glinda, the Good Witch of the North

CHAPTER 5

My knees give way. I slump to the ground.

"Put the kids in the car!"

"Oh my God!"

"Call an ambulance! Call the police!"

"Oh my God! Oh my God!"

I lie in the dirt, quivering. People screech, feet stomp, birds shriek, bees thunder and the wind howls. It is as if someone is hitting me between the eyes with a piece of slate. My head is going to burst.

Someone rips off my gag. I am moved onto my side. This opens up a small airway, enabling me to breathe somewhat. "Terrorists murdered Kristine," I say. There are bubbles in my voice.

A man's sweaty face comes close to mine. His breath is warm. It smells of marshmallows.

"Stay calm," he says. He unzips my fleece jacket. Icy air blasts my chest. "Bring me that cloth! Quick!"

A woman's voice is getting louder and faster. "Multiple stab wounds. Yes, yes, that's what I said. Bleeding badly. Ten minutes? You're kidding me! You have to get here quicker than that. She doesn't have ten minutes!"

The man with the sweet breath asks me what my name is and where Kristine is. I want to tell him that Kristine is hacked to death in the bushes. But I don't want to speak. I want everyone to go away. I want to die in peace.

But there is no peace.

"Kay, where is Kristine? Where is she?"

How can I say where she is? I don't know. All I know is the sun was behind me and I must have walked for about thirty minutes.

"West," I manage to say. "A mile."

He has deep worry lines in his forehead. How many terrorists were there? Did they have guns? Did you say two? Were there two?

My hands throb. My fingers are about to explode. Strewn on the ground a few inches away are my shoelaces caked in blood. I watch ants tunneling into the ground, trying to dodge stomping shoes. Few manage to find refuge.

I want to sleep. Yet I can't, because an icy wind lashes my skin. I shiver. Right in front of me, snow begins to fall. Within moments, flakes have formed a soft layer over crumpled leaves. Above me, icicles hang from frosty branches.

"She's going into shock!"

The trees, the sand, the table legs and the sky, everything is white with pale blue shadows. Just like winter, death has come too soon.

"Bring a blanket! Quick!"

The man tells me not to sleep, so I drag my eyelids open and focus on the wooden legs of the picnic table. I wish them ablaze, so that the wood will crackle and spit and send warming flames into the sky. But the cold grips me with icy and vicious fingers.

There is a new sound, whump, whump, whump. Soon it is as loud as a machine gun. Whump, whump, whump! I shift my eyes to look up. A helicopter is passing overhead. Monstrous and black, the blades slice the orange-streaked sky. It gets smaller. The thudding wanes, only to be replaced by a faint wail. Rising and falling, it crescendos into a banshee shriek.

"Ambulance! The ambulance is here!"

Brakes screech, gravel scatters and a concoction of hot rubber and exhaust fumes shoots up my nose. A stretcher opens next to me like a concertina. A man with a fuzzy black beard puts his hands on my hip. We're paramedics, he says. Another one, with a mop of ginger curls, tells me I'm safe and will be in hospital soon. I want him to speak again, because his breath is warm.

"One, two ..."

I am being impaled. Gulping for air and for anything, I am lifted four feet off the ground.

Peanut!

Bloodied and trembling, my puppy is cowering under the picnic table. I want to tell them, please, please, fetch her and put her in my arms. But I can't speak, so I tug at the curly-haired paramedic's sleeve and point.

"Is that your dog?" he asks. He leans in, close to my ear. "I'll come back to get her. I promise."

They push my stretcher into the ambulance. The doors slam. My little dog disappears.

The curly-haired paramedic is nowhere to be seen. The one with the bushy beard moves his finger back and forth in front of my eyes. I want water, but he tells me I can't have any. He says he's sorry about that. He is going to give me oxygen instead. It's better than water. It will make me feel good. He straps an oxygen mask to my face. The air is so cold it's hot. It singes my lungs. I don't mind; it's the only relief from the cold I have.

He slides a stethoscope over my chest. I watch his beard move when he talks. I don't need to worry. He is here to help. We will be there soon. He pulls the stethoscope from his ears and wipes the blood off the disc.

With every swerve of the ambulance, the siren howls, and what feels like iron stakes bore into my back. I am tossed from side to side like a piece of butchered meat. The bushy-bearded man tells me everything he is doing. He is going to check my blood pressure. It won't hurt. When he pumps, my arm swells and warmth rushes down to my fingers. Don't sleep, he keeps telling me, don't sleep. Velcro rips, air hisses and my fingers go cold again. He speaks into a walkie-talkie. When he talks the crackling stops. When he doesn't speak, the crackling starts.

"In her forties. Multiple stab wounds."

Crackle.

Stop. "Compound fractures."

Crackle.

Stop. "Critical."

He then says "Roger" and there is no more crackling.

"Don't sleep," he says, tapping his finger lightly on my cheek. "Don't sleep and don't speak. You mustn't speak. You mustn't close your eyes. Those are the two things you must not do. Can you remember that?"

Every time the vehicle swerves, I feel fluid swish around inside my chest. I must be drowning. I must be drowning in my own blood. But I don't care anymore. I just want to spend my last moments making peace with my Maker and thinking of those I love. Then, I want to sleep. I want to sleep forever and never wake up again.

"Toto, I've got a feeling we're not in Kansas anymore."

—Dorothy

CHAPTER 6

"Move out of the way!"

People slam themselves back against corridor walls as I am jostled down one dizzy passage after another. Above me lights blare, twisting, twirling, sucking me into the unknown. On the plastic mattress, my body slides around in a pool of blood.

"Clear the entrance!"

Teal collarless shirts and cotton surgical masks swarm around. Scissors snip, cutting through my fleece, down through my pants and underwear. The cool air stings my skin. There is a squelch as my clothes are stuffed into a plastic bag. Someone says "forensics."

Naked, I lie on a steel table so cold my skin must be stuck to it. I stare up at a sprawling metal mandrel clamped to the ceiling. This blinding light has two huge round dazzling bulbs and looks like a psychedelic tarantula.

There is a prick in my forearm. It feels as if my veins are being sucked dry. A man with a surgical mask leans over me. He smiles, his cheeks scrunching up and his dark eyes turning to slits. As he talks, his mask sucks in and out of his mouth.

What is your name? Where do you live? Do you have a phone number of family or friends? He furrows his eyebrows. It's alright, he tells me.

You're in good hands. You're in the Trauma Unit at Hadassah Hospital Ein Kerem in Jerusalem.

I say nothing, listening to the bubbling coming from my chest.

He pulls up my eyelids and moves his fingers across my face. "Fifteen," he says to no one in particular, and leaves.

Hands are suddenly all over my arms and legs, pinning me to the table. Another hand is pressing against my forehead. Fingers in latex gloves prod around my side. A man with bleached hair pulled back in a ponytail leans over me. In one hand he has an inch-wide plastic tube, in the other a scalpel. He inhales deeply, as if sucking on a joint, and says he is sorry it will hurt. There is no option. This has to be done right now, without anesthetic.

"Ready, guys?"

With the ease of riding a wave, the dude lances his scalpel into my side.

My eyeballs roll like marbles on a slanted tray. There is no air in my chest. A hot poker is being bored into my side. All I can do is listen to it squelch as he twists and turns it. I am being skewered alive.

* * *

A man with ruddy cheeks in a teal shirt holds what looks like a pistol over my chest.

"We need to staple up those stab wounds," he says, and bites his lip.

Without warning, he fires. Metal shoots into flesh. Snap. Crack. Tear. Rip. To cope with the pain, I count how many times he fires the gun. When I get to fifty-six, it stops. He takes off his blood-covered latex gloves.

"Get her to CT."

I am whizzed down a white corridor, into a gray elevator, down another white corridor into a dim room that contains what looks like a placed upright huge plastic doughnut ring. Beside it are two men. One has floppy bangs and the other is bald and holds a clipboard. The hairy one tells me they are the technicians. They need to do some scanning. To do the scanning they need to move me onto the couch.

The couch.

He makes it sound so comfortable. But the couch next to the hole in the doughnut is nothing but a metal bench covered with a thin blue sheet.

"One, two ..."

Colored prisms dance behind my eyes. When they finally disappear, I find myself lying in a dim tunnel. It is a quiet space, without pounding footsteps, the clanging of metal and people shouting. All I can hear is an occasional click and a faraway voice telling me to lie still. I stare up at the curved ceiling. I want to stay here until I die.

And then I am out of the tunnel. The man with the bangs covers me with a sheet and lays a clipboard on my stomach. I am again whizzed down corridors, this time into a small, quiet room. To my side, about ten feet away, are double doors with two round smoked-glass windows. They look like eyes with cataracts. Above them is a sign. In Hebrew, Arabic and English, it says "Operating Theater."

A slender nurse with chocolate skin and black eyes comes through the doors and tucks my hair under a plastic shower cap. She pulls the sheet up to my chin and tells me that there is a policeman here who needs to talk to me. It won't take long, she promises. She smiles and blinks many times, then turns her back and busies herself with the bags of liquids hanging on the poles.

Someone coughs. I look down past my feet. Hovering at the end of the bed is a policeman, his cap casting a shadow over the top half of his face. He shifts his weight from one foot to another as if waiting for a signal to start. The nurse tells him to be quick. He edges closer until he is standing beside my head. He stoops down to my face. In broken English, he says, "What. Your. Name?"

My tongue is stuck to my palate. When I try to speak, it peels away, releasing a noxious stench. It makes him turn his head away. He coughs, tips the rim of his cap, then asks the same question again.

"Her name is Wilson," says the nurse in Hebrew. "Kay Wilson. They established that upon her arrival. Why don't you ask her about ..."

My nose is itchy. I lift the oxygen mask to scratch it. Suddenly, it feels as if someone in high heels is stomping across my chest. I gulp for air.

"You mustn't touch the mask," the nurse says, putting it back in place. Air seeps in and the stampede stops. Her eyes flash at the policeman. "The ranger is also waiting to see her before she goes in to theater. You have to do this quickly."

He promises her in Hebrew that he will be quick. Turning to me, he reverts to English.

"Kay. You. A-m-e-r-i-c-a?"

Why is he speaking in English, and why is every syllable a sentence, and why is he asking if I am American? Too irked to bother with "I was born in …," I manage to say, "England."

He chews his pen and squeezes out his next question.

"What. Friend. Name?"

I say her name.

"Luken? Hmm. Kristine, England?"

I shake my head

"Hmm. Kristine, A-m-e-r-i-c-a?"

I nod.

"What. Your. Hotel?"

That he thinks I live in a hotel is as bewildering for me as his practicing his painful English.

"You. Have. Number?"

I am so near to death, I can hardly talk. I just want him to go so I can die. Still, I can only die in peace if I tell him a phone number. The only two numbers I remember are those of the car tow company and that of my friend, Hannah. Hers is easy. The digits are all in order. Because I only remember numbers in Hebrew, I say it in his mother tongue.

His face lights up. "Your. Hebrew. Beautiful!" He thanks me in Hebrew, and just to be sure that I understand him, thanks me again in

English. On the way out, I hear him tell the nurse that she is to wish me health, happiness, long life – and a good time in Israel.

* * *

Where the policeman stood is now a hulk of a man with a jaw so square it could have been cut from limestone. He has tree-trunk thighs and rocky biceps. The only part of him that is anything less than mammoth are his flinty eyes. Under the ridge of his cliff-like brow they look like small caves. Rather incongruously, this giant wears a fluffy, pea-green fleece jacket.

In a deep voice, he tells me his name is Gidi Bashan. He is the ranger of the Matta Forest. He unfolds a map and clasps it under his chin. His nose is flat and wide enough for an afternoon stroll.

He points to the bottom left corner of the map. "Here is where you parked the car. Here is where they found you. And you came from here."

With each "here" he drags a chunky finger across the map. All I have to do is signal – move my thumb up for yes, down for no. Is that good? Can I do that for him? I squint. The map is all a blur. He shuffles closer and asks me to let him know when I can see it more clearly.

"Was this the route you walked with Kristine?"

I raise my thumb, yes.

"Tell me about the walk, Kay. Were you stopping and chatting?"

I signal yes again.

Not taking his eyes off me, he asks for how long we walked: an hour, fifty minutes, forty? I signal at thirty.

Did you pass the place that had been cordoned off for saplings?

Thumb up.

Did you reach the crossroad leading down to the Roman steps?

Thumb up.

Where did you go then, he asks. Because this question has neither a yes nor a no answer, I don't know what to do. His voice is tight.

47

"Kay, there are four hundred police, soldiers, volunteers and dogs looking for Kristine. I need to know where you went. We have to rule out a kidnapping."

The mention of kidnapping makes me feel as if I am falling. Stay with me, I hear him say. Stay with me, just another thirty seconds. Thirty seconds, Kay, just thirty seconds.

Did you go down the steps?

Thumb down.

Did you walk west, towards the sun?

Thumb down.

He frowns. It looks as if he spends his whole life thinking. Then he asks if we could see Beit Shemesh from where we were.

"It's important, Kay. Try to remember."

He moves his thumb up and down, urging me to make a choice. I raise my thumb. Energized, he gives the air a punch. "If you could see Beit Shemesh, that means you and Kristine must have climbed up to the lookout. You can't see Beit Shemesh from anywhere else!"

Beit Shemesh.

I want to tell him that when we were standing at the top of the hill, Kristine said that the sun striking the high-rise balconies made the shadows look like piano keys.

But he has gone.

* * *

Warm and weightless, I float in a space with green walls. It feels as if I am in an aquarium. Above me, oval ceiling lights shine down, warming my skin. Two men sit on stools on either side of me. One is thin and pale, with charcoal rings under his eyes. He looks as if he has spent decades in the gulags. The other is dark-skinned, with sooty eyes and tortoise-shelled glasses. Both men wear teal bandannas and latex gloves. They fiddle with tweezers, needles and pliers on trays and chat about goat cheese.

"Making *labane*, dear Vladimir," says the darker man, "is as straightforward as this keyhole surgery. Just add cumin. You know what they say about cumin." He chuckles to himself. "The more pungent the better."

The tired man sighs a little *Oy*.

"Obviously I haven't got that Arab touch," he says in Russian-accented Hebrew. "Tell your Aisha to give me a call. You said she has a reputation for making the best *labane* in all of Jerusalem."

The doctor who likes lots of cumin peers over at me. I catch sight of my face reflected in his glasses. Etched into my cheeks are long, deep grazes. My nose is purple and on my forehead is a welt partly covered by the shower cap over my hair.

"Count backwards," he says.

I don't want to count backwards. Scared to never wake up again, I fight to keep my eyes open. My eyelids feel like they are being tethered down to my cheeks by tent pegs. An arm stretches across me, blocking out the light from above.

There is a glint of steel and a man says,

"Mohammed, pass me that knife."

"Pardon me. That way is a very nice way."

—**Scarecrow**

CHAPTER 7

White and gray swirl around me. The hues materialize into a woman, a large woman with a broad bosom above a belly that resembles stacked tires. Her hair is pulled back in a bun and streaked at the roots. She tells me her name is Olga. She is a nurse and she is going to take care of me.

Nurse Olga presses a button on the side of the bed, raising the top and bringing me up into a sitting position.

"You've had an operation," she says. "You have to stay sitting up. Dying of pneumonia after all you've been through would be ridiculous."

She adjusts the tube clipped to my nostrils and removes a pillow from behind my back. After a couple of whumps and thumps she puts it back. Unbuttoning my pajamas, she reveals a thick pink wad attached to my chest. She picks at the edges of the tape holding it in place, lifts up the pad and wipes around colored wires attached to my chest. The wiping cotton smells of vodka. It turns pink before my eyes.

While she puts on a new dressing, Olga chats away. "The knife missed your heart by a hair's breadth, sweetie. Not to worry, though, you're in the best place. Did you know that the cardiology ward in Hadassah Ein Kerem is the pinnacle of Israeli medicine? Hearts are my specialty. I've worked here since I came to Israel many years ago and wouldn't work anywhere else. Not everyone gets to be a patient here.

There's a waiting list. You're a very lucky girl." She looks at me happily, encouraging me to soak up my achievement.

Olga exhales a little "ooh" of joy and gives my cheek a squeeze. Nurse Olga and I are magnet and steel.

I'm not allowed to drink, not at the moment. But, thinking that my lips need a little moisture, she dips a cube of sponge into a glass of water and squeezes it over my mouth. Droplets seep into the ravines on my lips. The water feels divine. She does it again. I catch the drops with my tongue and lick around my mouth, making sure none is wasted.

"Alright then," she sighs, reluctantly. "But just to wet your tongue. Promise?"

When she puts the glass to my lips, I bite the edge so she can't take it away. I gulp. Horses gallop over my sternum. I am being crushed to death. Frowning, Nurse Olga waits with me for the stampede to pass.

"See!" she says indignantly. "I told you not to do that. You can only drink when the doctor says it is alright to do so."

Appropriately scolded, I look away and eye the tube poking out from under the sheet on my left side that leads down to a clear plastic container filled with maroon sludge on the floor. The nurse watches my eyes.

"That, my dear, is a depository. It's the drainage from your lungs. The tube has to stay in until your lungs are clear." Nurse Olga says I don't need to worry about anything. Oh, she adds, she has something just for emergencies.

"Hold out your hand." She presses a rubber ball into my palm. It has a wire coming out of it that disappears behind the headboard.

"The morphine you're getting intravenously should be enough, but if you're in too much pain, you can squeeze this. It releases that little bit extra of what you need. You can't overdose, but it may make you feel sick or dizzy. It could also make you happy." She corrects herself. "Not happy, exactly. You may feel sort of lightheaded, floating and relaxed. You have to rest now. Doctor's orders. You will need all your strength very soon."

She draws the curtain around my bed and leaves. I begin to drift. Soon I am floating in the calm blue Mediterranean Sea. Not entirely treading water, I bob up and down, occasionally making sure I can touch the sea floor with my toe. I like to know it is there.

Suddenly, I can't feel the bottom. I kick my legs frantically until I come up and gasp for air.

It is my mind that kicks and struggles, grasping for anything to stop me sinking into the deep. My thoughts lunge for the window. Through it I see a building, not all the building, just the top. It is covered with panes of glass that reflect blue skies with feathery clouds.

My thoughts race.

With all that glass, it must be so hot inside. Muggy hot. Desert hot. Humid hot. Radiation hot. Boiling hot. Melting hot. Matches. Lighters. Ovens. Sun. Kettles. Irons. Chili peppers. Coffee. All are hot.

When I have exhausted heat, I grasp for something else. On top of the building are antennas, but there are no chimneys. Israel doesn't have chimneys because Israel doesn't have fireplaces. Israel should have fireplaces because houses are too cold in winter. Freezing cold. Foggy cold. Bitterly cold. Chilly cold. Icy cold. Other things are cold too. Ice cream. The snow in the Golan Heights, and the Banias Waterfall. Fridges are cold. Pluto. Winter Olympics. Flu. All of these are cold. The cold makes my heart pound, so I look beyond the buildings. The Jerusalem hills dotted with pines. The beeps of the monitor begin to speed up as my heart thumps fast and hard. Only when I turn my eyes away from the trees, do the beeps and my heart slow down.

Think. I have to think. My eyes settle on the contents in the depository. It looks like raspberry jelly.

Jelly.

Jelly, jelly, jelly. I say it again, ten times, twenty times. I love how the word sounds. Raspberry jelly, plum jelly, blackberry jelly, blueberry jelly, mango jelly, apple jelly. Orange jelly is too sweet. It's not real marmalade. Israel should have real marmalade. Someone should import the stuff. When I finish constructing a business plan to import marmalade, I turn my attention to the catheter.

Yellow.

Bananas, chicks, corn, roses, sunflowers, canaries, tennis balls, ice cream ... I count fourteen things that are yellow. Fifteen, when I remember lemon drops.

Lemon drops.

Where trouble melts like lemon drops away above the chimney tops.

I wrack my brain. Of course I know it! It's from my favorite movie. I decide I am going to play every scene of *The Wizard of Oz* in my mind, starting from boring old Kansas, to Dorothy being swept into the Land of Oz by the tornado. What a journey she had, skipping along the Yellow Brick Road arm in arm with her companions, Scarecrow, Tin Man and Cowardly Lion. Dorothy's little Kansas dress is the same blue as the curtain drawn around my bed. My eyes drift lazily into its folds. Blue is so calming and so everywhere. It's not just Dorothy's dress, it's the seas, it's the skies, it's the—

"I'm so sorry I'm so sorry I'm so sorry I'm so sorry ..."

I turn my head. How cool! My friend Hannah is sitting beside my bed. She must have magically appeared through Dorothy's little blue dress. She grabs my hand and strokes it ferociously. She keeps saying, I'm so sorry I'm so sorry I'm so sorry. Her voice sounds as if it's about to snap. Her eyes are puffy and her cheeks are tear-stained and she inhales so deeply that her chest rises like a pumped balloon. She fingers the cuff of my pajamas. Her bracelet has little pink beads. Flamingo pink. Flamingos. I should ask her if she wants to go to Eilat and see the flamingos at the salt ponds. I love flamingos.

She locks her fingers around mine.

"They've found Kristine's body."

She flings her face into the mattress and sobs. I, on the other hand, let my eyes drift up to the curtain rings. I count them. First in Hebrew, then in English. If I'm not mistaken, there are 48. Hang on, though, I thought I counted 98. It can't be. Double 48 is 96, not 98. I must count again. Each time I count I come up with a different number. I can't concentrate. With her incessant "I'm so sorry I'm so sorry" and never-ending howling, Hannah is disturbing me. How very inconsiderate.

Finally, she stops. Thank God for that. Now I can listen to the sweet beeps of the monitor in peace. But the beeps sound like cheeps. Cheep cheep cheep. Birds. Little birds. Little birds ... Birds! Birds! My pulse races. Little birds singing in the forest.

I have to think of anything but birds. The jagged lines moving across the monitor look like the rim of the Ramon Crater. What a place! I love to take my tourists there. Once I even told a friend from America with green-

54

blue eyes and an infectious laugh that you can stand with your toes on the edge, hovering over the abyss. The crater is immense, naked and hostile, I told her. It's God's pilot version of the Grand Canyon. Her eyes widened when I told her that people have plunged to their deaths there because of a sudden gust of the dry and dusty eastern wind. But she soon laughed when I told her that there was only one warning sign: *Do not feed the ibex.* Israel makes people think for themselves.

Thinking of her makes blood pound in my ears. Everything is muffled. I can just make out Hannah saying, "Doctor! Where's the doctor?" In rushes a man in a white coat. His face is pale and he has raccoon-dark circles under his eyes. Wiping her nose with a ragged tissue, Hannah asks him if I'll be alright. He answers her in Hebrew with a thick Russian accent, with all the zest needed to read out a bus schedule.

"It's to be expected. She has thirteen machete lacerations in her lungs and diaphragm, six open compound fractures of her ribs, and some of the bones have splintered into the lungs. Her sternum is broken in two places. The knife missed her aorta by four millimeters, and that lung drain, well, what can I say? It's a very painful business."

Hannah nods a lot and says, uh huh, uh huh. The Russian continues.

"Repairing the tears in her diaphragm was not a complex procedure in itself, but because of her punctured lung, it was high risk. You'll be glad to know that Dr. Mohammed did a magnificent job."

"Mohammed?" titters Hannah.

"Not only is he the best of all our Arab doctors, he's one of the best surgeons in Israel."

He continues. "The breaks are complex. There are about thirty in all. Her right shoulder is dislocated and her shoulder blade is broken. It must be said that it's quite a feat to break a shoulder blade. On average, a human bone can sustain forty times the amount of force that concrete can. Of course, that is an average and not specific to the scapula or the age of a person, but it's safe to say, she was beaten with a brute force rarely even seen from the Russian mafia."

He gives his stethoscope a little polish with his sleeve. "It will take a long time. She'll be in a lot of pain, but with friends like you and a good bit of morphine, she should pull through."

* * *

The wires on my chest feed into a machine that gives off a suffused hum like the thrum of a plane. Nurse Olga pulls back the curtain with the debonair confidence of a flight attendant and gives me a little look as if to apologize for the riffraff in economy.

"I'm sorry, my love. The guard needs to see you. He's a nice chap. I told him he should threaten to shoot the journalists in the kneecaps if they won't go away."

Journalists? Why are journalists here? And what's with a guard? I imagine the watchman. He must be tough, most likely the strong and silent type who draws a gun without blinking an eye and chews gum while he takes a shot. He probably has greased black hair and a scar down his face.

I don't have to wonder too long about what kind of man would shoot reporters in the kneecaps, because he walks, or rather shuffles, into the room and towards the bed. He looks to be in his late twenties and he is wearing the same kind of shirt worn by security men who pace around the airport looking for unattended, suspicious bags. Around his ear is a curly white chord. By the way his eyelids droop and the stubble on his chin, it looks as if this guy has not slept a wink in days.

"Hello," he says, sleepily.

"Hello," I say.

He looks at his shoes. "How are you?"

"I'm fine."

Still looking at his shoes, he says he is fine too. He says he didn't want to disturb me, he just wanted to say hello and tell me he's got my back. He's here if I need anything. It's amazing how many journalists want to see me, he tells his shoes. For three years he worked as a bodyguard for politicians from both the Likud and the Labor parties, and in all that time he never saw journalists taking such an interest in them as they are in me. Just shows how the politicians are all so irrelevant, don't I think?

He looks up. He had better get back.

I nod. Vigorously.

With his holster sagging over his withered butt, he heads towards his job.

* * *

There are roadwork noises in my head and my jaw is being jerked from side to side. Ice-mint air burns my mouth. Hannah holds up a toothbrush smeared in froth.

She hands me a paper cup. "Rinse, please."

I spit. Then I hold the cup to my ear. Over the fizzle of my saliva, I hear Hannah's muffled voice. She is saying that my friend Mira called my family in England and told them what had happened. She says I'll be able to have visitors as soon as the police are finished with me. It's nothing to worry about, she keeps saying. What's most important, I am alive. I press the cup harder against my ear. Over the sound of waves washing against rocks, I hear Hannah saying she'll buy me new glasses and sneakers. Pink laces, pink rubber soles, just like my other ones. Don't worry about your family, the police, or anything else, she says.

Her words spill out at breakneck speed.

"I've made a list of people to help. Shoshi, Mona, Orit, Miriam, Mira, Liat, Stephanie, Linda, Orna, Dafna, Gila and Tami have all put their names down. Skinny wanted to do a night watch. But I told him 'girls only.' Is that alright with you?" She blows her nose. "Mona asked me if she can watch the 'The Bold and the Beautiful,' when she comes at the end of the week. A television will be nice for the people doing their shifts, don't you think? It will also take your mind off things. Did I mention that I've ordered new glasses for you? As soon as Ari gets leave from the army, he'll come too. Mira told your mother you have plenty of friends who are going to look after you. It's best if she comes over from England when you're out of the hospital. There's no point her being here now. Not knowing Hebrew, she'll feel helpless, don't you think? She seemed relieved. Anyway, I have to go. I still have work to do, and the babysitter charges a fortune."

In a flat voice, Hannah asks if I heard anything she said. I say I did, but I don't know if that's true. I turn my head to the window. The glass panes in the building are charcoal gray. The hills are wrapped in purple sheets. It's almost night outside.

* * *

I dream about a company of bald-headed dwarfs, who under the command of my dog Peanut plant sunflower seeds in the Negev Desert. It's all very pleasant. When I wake up, there is a man with a bald head who has his face in my cleavage.

Holding a small camera an inch from my chest, his breath tickles my skin. I stare at the specks of sweat on his shiny scalp, then look over at Nurse Olga fidgeting with the drips at the side of the bed. Her hair is pulled back tight. It resembles an onion. I love onions. I love how they feel all papery on the outside, and when the skin is peeled off, they become cool and hard. I can't eat too many onions though, they make me burp.

Nurse Olga adjusts the valves and chats away. "This gentleman is from the Institute of Forensic Medicine in Holon. Have you been to Holon, Kay? That's where the Jewish Agency had the nerve to put us when we arrived in Israel. In those days, Holon wasn't any more friendly than the Kremlin. We even—"

"Nurse," says the man, taking his head out of my chest. "Can you take off Kay's pajamas please, so I can get to her back?"

While Nurse Olga eases my top off, the man looks past me at the lamp on the headboard. His lips are thick, his forehead high, and his eyes bulge. He gives his best smile and tells me his name is Avi. He doesn't look like an Avi though, he looks like an explorer, or a philosopher, or a scientist.

Einstein. I'll call him Einstein.

Einstein, who seconds ago had his face in my cleavage, now thanks me in a formal voice for my cooperation and apologizes for the intrusion.

I edge forward so he can get to my back. Even moving a couple of inches brings on the agony of feeling impaled. He grimaces with me and waits for my pain to subside, then embarks on his scientific expedition. He documents what he calls "lacerations." It sounds exciting. He has an efficient but mysterious method. It involves a tape measure, the camera and a clipboard. Working his way down my side and across my back, he mutters secret formulas to himself, like "two-and-a-half inches," as if worried he may forget.

He gives the camera a couple of clicks, puts it down, hurriedly writes on the clipboard and then goes back to the tape measure. It is clammy on my skin and makes me shudder. Camera clicks. Pen scratches. Camera clicks. Pen scratches.

Genius. I am in the presence of genius.

Engrossed in his mission, Einstein gives me the feeling that he is working on something that will change the world. I wonder what it could be. Whatever it is, I feel quite proud to be part of this great experiment, even though it means being photographed naked from the waist up.

Nurse Olga resumes her monologue about how, back in the '90's, Holon used to be a real dump. But, genius that he is, Einstein is too consumed with his world-breaking discovery. He just says, "Nurse, let me concentrate for a moment, please."

I blink around the room. Einstein must have been so excited at what he discovered that he slipped away without saying goodbye, to carry on working towards his great invention. Olga's not here anymore either. She must have gone with him.

All is the same here in my little blue room – except for my pajamas. They're bigger than the ones I was wearing when Einstein was here. The sleeves even cover the tips of my fingers, and they smell like a baby's warm head. If I focus hard enough I can even read the label on the collar.

Cotton garments. To be washed at 30 degrees Celsius. Full wash load for a maximum 120 minutes. Always dry on a low heat.

Einstein wrote that. It's a secret formula. I know it.

"What's all this jabber-wapping when there's work to be done?"

—Aunty Em

CHAPTER 8

I feel as if I have been staring into Officer Lilach's warm kind eyes for years.

"Who wanted water?" she says.

"The men in the bushes."

"Did you know them?"

"Know them? Why would I?"

She asks what they looked like.

To make her laugh, when I describe them, I furrow my eyebrows and snarl.

"Both were ugly as hell," I add.

Lilach narrows her eyes. "Kay, are you saying that the one with the police jacket and army pants had bad teeth, and the one with the dirty gray jacket had funny eyebrows? Is that what you are saying?"

She says it's a good description, but it would be even better if I could expand on it. What exactly do I mean by "bad teeth" and "funny eyebrows?" Can I tell her more? Even if I think something is unimportant, Lilach wants me to tell her everything.

My lips are split and so dry and sore that speaking widens the cracks. Forbidden to drink or swallow, all I can do is try to moisten them with a tongue that is as dry as my lips. On the bedside cabinet and just out of my reach is the glass of water and the little cube of yellow sponge. Nurse Olga put them there so that, as she put it, I don't drink and kill myself. That glass serves exclusively for "lip dabbing," she warned. I watch that sponge bobbing inside.

Reading my mind, Officer Lilach hands me the glass.

"Remember, doctor's orders. No swallowing," she says.

I squeeze the sponge. Water fills the cracks in my lips like a flash flood in the Zanoah Brook. It is so good it is celestial.

"I stabbed one," I say.

"You stabbed one?"

"Yeah. Not hard, though. My penknife is one of those small ones."

Officer Gil wants to know where I stabbed the man.

"In the nuts."

"With which hand?"

"Right."

At some point, I mention that the men smoked and spoke on the phone. For the police, this information is as important as the penknife.

"I think it was Marlboro," I say. "Or … I dunno … maybe it was L&M Red. I don't remember. All I know is that at that moment I would have paid a million shekels for a cigarette."

The phone calls, the cigarettes, my stabbing the man in the nuts, all make Officer Gil's eyeballs bulge. Unexpectedly, a funny little memory pops up in my mind, of when I dissected a sheep's eyeball in science class in junior high school. When I lanced it with the scalpel, the eyeball skidded across the table and plopped onto the floor with a squelch.

Lilach asks me if I could hear what they were saying on the phone.

"I couldn't understand much," I say, trying not to laugh. "It was something about waiting for a car. You should have seen Kristine's face. It was like this."

I cover my mouth with my hand to demonstrate the gag and widen my eyes until they sting.

Lilach takes my wrist and gently moves my hand away.

"Everything is helpful, Kay," she says, softly.

I am about to burst with pride. "Gee, thanks, Lilach. Anyway, back on point, after about half an hour one stabbed me loads of times while the other hacked up Kristine in front of my eyes."

Oh my God! What a sight! Lilach's pupils are like forming galaxies. If I look hard enough, I can see black skies with sparkling trees, happy little blue birds and pretty pink and yellow lights. It is so beautiful. I am about to burst out of my skin with joy.

It is time for music.

Cue "Somewhere Over the Rainbow."

This little song of jubilation I play on my make-believe tuba, pam-pa-ing through the first line with rubbery and vibrating lips. But a few lines in, I forget the rest of the tune. It doesn't matter because the police don't seem to be enjoying it anyway. They stare at their laps and look morose. Such a shame. Oz is a wonderful place.

"He said, 'Oilcan!'"

—Scarecrow

CHAPTER 9

I scurry my fingers yet again over my stomach, imagining it to be a piano. I must have played "Somewhere Over the Rainbow" on my "tummy piano" at least a thousand times today, or maybe it's tonight. Yes, it's tonight. Day is the blue skies reflected in the glass building. Night is the silky velvet purple hills. I don't care when it is, the song is always beautiful to me. I imagine my fingers are placed over those of my favorite pianist, the late, chubby black Canadian, Oscar Peterson. Oscar always amazed me: How did such a big man have so much dexterity in his fingers? With his crescendos, diminuendos, mellow yet complex harmonies, he made the piano sound like an entire orchestra.

But, out of character, Oscar is speaking while he is playing, and he is doing so in Hebrew.

"Hi Kay, my name is Oscar."

Strangely, Oscar is a skinny white guy with jug ears and a bad haircut. It can't be Oscar. Oscar Peterson speaks English, not Hebrew.

I scratch my head. "Do you play the piano?"

"You know how it is," he sighs. "The years just slip by."

Because he seems regretful, I tell him it's never too late to start. It's good to begin with the right technique. When I lift my arm to demonstrate this "right technique," what feels like a harpoon skewers me through the chest.

"Ouch," says Oscar.

Ouch, I think, wondering if this is it: Am I about to die?

Oscar drags up the plastic chair and takes a seat beside me. "I'm sorry we had to come at this hour of the night."

"We? Who is we?"

One by one, five men with leather jackets, buzz-cut hair, and Ray-Bans appear through the blue curtain into the cubicle. They can't be doctors. Doctors always come in the morning and wear white coats. And what's with the sunglasses? It's dark outside.

One wearing sunglasses with orange frames tells me, thank you.

"You're welcome," I say.

He stands behind Oscar. Three others take their positions opposite them. The last man stands at the end of the bed, his back to me. I catch sight of a pistol poking out of a holster on his belt. Behind his ear is a squiggly chord, the kind the guard has, the guard who one day may shoot a journalist in the kneecaps.

Oscar hands me a clipboard. By signing this, I agree not to speak about this conversation with anyone. By the look in his narrowed eyes, he means it.

He lowers his voice. "Kay, the Shin Bet needs your help."

The Shin Bet? The Israeli Security Agency? I can hardly believe it! No one knows who they are, yet here they are with little ol' me who has never so much as thrown a punch, and we're on a first-name basis! What a trip!

Dizzy with intrigue, I gaze at Agent Oscar, and wonder what missions he has been up to in life. Probably bumped off some Nazis. Probably assassinated a few terrorists. Probably spied on Iran. Probably done missions on every continent. Wide-eyed, I try to guess the names of the others. Agent Marksman, Agent Hitman, Agent Scarface, Agent Cohen and Agent Bond.

Thoughts race about my future with the agency. Espionage, reconnaissance, undercover and intrigue, the stuff that movies are made of! It must be because I have dual citizenship, or because I'm bilingual, or perhaps both. No one would ever know I am Israeli.

Oscar makes a point of looking at his watch. "When you are ready, Kay, please sign the State Secrecy Act."

Not wanting to come across as too eager, I keep my face nonchalant and sign with indifference. But inside, excitement tingles. Who knows where I will be sent? Maybe to Europe, or South America. Lots of Nazis fled to Argentina. Or maybe that's the Mossad who takes care of that, not the Shin Bet? Damn it! I can't remember.

Enlisted and ready for mission, I await my instructions from Agent Oscar. But Oscar isn't in a hurry. He stares into space grinding his jaw. Finally, he says,

"We need you to look at some photos."

Photos? I try to read his face, but he gives nothing away.

Agent Marksman hands me a white folder with black print. On the cover it says,

"Kristine Luken Murder. December 18, 2010."

Like magic, black and white swirl and dance, resolving into piano keys. I take the top octaves while Oscar Peterson tackles the lower register of the piano. The musical genius stretches his fingers and forms a G flat major with an octave flattened fifth in the bass. Swing based, syncopated rhythm, he plays an embellished harmony while I tinker an improvised melody. Overplay and underplay, Peterson sticks in a couple of lovely tritones – that's always a great trick for refreshing a tired phrase. Just as he turns into the second refrain, he disappears, banished by a dull gallop that is irritatingly out of time.

In place of Oscar Peterson, there is a thin white man with jug ears and hair that looks like it was cut with a bowl over his head, rapping his fingers on the bedside cabinet.

"No one will hurt you," he says. He looks around at his colleagues. No one will, says the guy with the orange sunglasses. No one at all, they all chime in.

With sweaty hands, I open the file. My stomach is already in my mouth. Because I am going to pass out, or throw up, I close it again.

"I don't know if I can do this."

Oscar doesn't flinch. "Yes you can, Kay. Just remember the worst is over."

The photos are all mugshots. Pages and pages of mugshots. There are untamed thugs with scarred flesh, black-bearded beasts with cracked lips, and sallow-cheeked rogues with stubbled chins. Along with the bad and the ugly are some who are cute or even drop-dead gorgeous. Clean-shaven chaps with clear olive skin. Well-groomed fellows with firm, square jaws. Pleasant men, aspiring men, men who could be bankers, doctors or entrepreneurs.

And then—

I see a single joined eyebrow in one photo and then another shot of rat-like ears and yellow teeth, wedged unevenly into salmon gums. Wanting to obliterate their faces from my sight, I press my finger so hard into the page my finger goes white.

Oscar pries the folder out of my hands.

"We'll get the bastards," he says, his jaw determined. "I promise you, Kay. We'll get them."

* * *

Two men with padded black bags slung over their shoulders come in to my space. Unlike my last visitors, these guys have hair everywhere. One is stocky, with fuzzy white hair at the sides of his head like David Ben-Gurion, Israel's first prime minister. Unlike Ben-Gurion though, he also has black hair sprouting out of his nostrils. The other man, who is skinny and pasty-faced, has tangled ringlets lurching for freedom out of the neck of his T-shirt.

Hair is everywhere. It is all over the place.

They unzip their bags and take out cables, metal stands, black gadgets, microphones and cameras. This won't take long, Ben-Gurion says, and smiles only with the right side of his mouth.

I want to ask what won't take long, but feel a bit embarrassed, because they act as if I was expecting them. They seem so at home, as if we had an appointment. I don't want to seem stupid or forgetful, so I just say OK.

Ben-Gurion fiddles with the furred microphone, which looks like a small head of hair. Pasty shuffles around with a camera lodged on his shoulder, muttering about "angles," "cuts," and "shots." He is wearing frayed jeans that are too long and catch under his old sneakers. When he reaches over my head to plug in a lead, a waft of stale armpit seeps up my nostrils. The plug doesn't fit. He keeps trying to push it in, while asking me how I am, thanking me for the interview and apologizing for the inconvenience. All the while, his armpit is in my face. The smell makes me want to throw up, so I think of the pink-tinted landscapes of the Negev Desert, where even atheists say their prayers.

Success.

Fresh air.

Then the guard comes in. He looks at the men.

"Kay's friend is outside. He parked his bus on a red line, because there wasn't anywhere else he could leave it. He needs to be quick because he doesn't want to get a ticket. He needs to come in for just a couple of minutes."

Ben-Gurion sounds as if he has trodden on a rotting lizard.

"For God's sake," he rants. "I don't need one more person in here. There's barely enough room. I've been cooped up on a bench in the waiting room for two days. I haven't slept a wink. Doesn't he have the manners to wait? This won't take more than twenty minutes. Bus drivers make more money than we do. He can afford a parking ticket. Why now? Alright, alright, let him in."

As the guard walks out, he turns around and gives me a "we're in this together" thumbs-up. I like him. Although he probably still would not shoot anyone in the kneecaps, he does have a sense of mischief about him.

In comes Khalil Nazari. And his wife. And his twin brother. And his brother's wife.

* * *

Khalil mops sweat from his brow and tucks his handkerchief into the pocket of his pinstriped navy suit. It's unusual for Khalil to sweat; he avoids going outside unnecessarily into the burning sun. When we're with a tour group, he barely leaves the bus. He has his usual list of lame excuses. He knows the sites. He's seen them before. He prefers to stay in the air-conditioned bus.

There was one time, however, when he did leave the bus, and he dripped with perspiration.

Like all of Israel's summers, that August was sweltering. Khalil and I were taking a family of seven on a tour of Israel: a good-humored father with an impressive vocal range; his personable wife, who sang with him in harmony; their two amiable daughters and their equally never-get-ruffled husbands, and finally the only grandchild, five-year old Charlie, who had yellow bangs that hung over blue eyes and who would stay up beyond his bedtime so as not miss out on family singsongs. Khalil remarked, "They remind me of that movie about that Austrian musical family, in World War Two, you know, the one with the nun, who by singing together escaped from the Nazis."

While on the bus, the group serenaded us. To a rousing chorus of "Swing Low, Sweet Chariot," we chugged up from the Dead Sea to our clifftop lodgings in the desert village of Mitzpeh Yericho.

I hopped off the bus to learn that a water pipe had just burst at our booked accommodation, flooding the place and making our staying there implausible. It was Friday evening. The Sabbath had already begun. Everything was closed. Observant Jews were at synagogue.

With our group's affection and enthusiasm wilting after a long day under the desert sun, the singing stopped and worry lines broke out on foreheads.

That's when Khalil got off the bus and started to sweat.

Taking command, he went one way looking for help, while I went the other. In his suit, his burly frame paced the dusty streets. After searching unsuccessfully for about twenty minutes, I headed, worried, back to the bus.

I needn't have worried.

Sitting under a pergola overlooking the Jordan Valley, Khalil and our group were tucking into watermelon. With them was a clean-shaven man with a black yarmulke. A woman in a calf-length dress was bringing plates of chicken, salad, and potatoes to the table. Khalil patted the empty chair beside him and beckoned me to sit down.

His new friends, Rabbi Uri and his wife, "the lovely Aliza," had offered for everyone to stay at their house. For free. Including meals. Everything was taken care of. He gave me a wink.

And with that, the rabbi and the Arab resumed their passionate discussion about the weekly Bible portion.

When we left a couple of days later, Khalil told the rabbi that as a tour bus driver there was not a hotel in Israel he had not been to, but this was the nicest place he had ever stayed. This he said, while accepting two large boxes of cake and fruit from the lovely Aliza.

* * *

Proud, portly and in that same pinstripe suit, Khalil sticks his thumbs in his belt and orders the women to clear the bedside cabinet to make space.

"It's *baklava*," Khalil says, "homemade." He gives me his familiar, knowing, don't-you-worry-about-anything, protective wink, the one he gives when we get stuck in traffic with a tour group and he diverts to the back roads (so narrow that he almost scrapes the mirrors) to save time and stay on schedule with our itinerary. It's the wink of "everything is under control." It's the wink of Mitzpeh Yericho, the wink that makes me feel relieved.

Khalil turns to the film crew. "Please, gentlemen, pretend we are not here."

Ben-Gurion puts on a spongy pair of earphones and tinkers with a small metal box attached to his belt. Legs astride, Pasty lodges the camera on his shoulder and stands at the end of the bed, a few feet off to the right.

"Ready to go ahead, Kay?" he says. "Can you tell us about what happened in the forest?"

A red light flashes on the top of his camera.

I don't remember where my glasses are. I always have my glasses. Truth be told, my hair could probably also do with a brushing, but I don't say so. Just my glasses will do, please.

"You look fine without them," he says. He takes a step towards me. My chest tightens, my breath speeds up.

Khalil's voice is icy. "Move back, right now."

For several moments, the two men try to outstare each other. Pasty concedes and takes a step back.

As soon as it begins, it's over. Talking to the media proves to be as effortless as it was surprising. I find I can speak about the events with lucidity and coherence. It is not an out-of-body experience or even a way-up-high experience. It isn't planned. It just happens.

And this is how.

In the interview, whenever I say certain words, my brain suddenly leaps to something else related to that word. When I say, "They stole my identity card," my mind jumps from the word "identity" to the word "identical" and then to "identical twin" and that leads me to think about Khalil, because Khalil is an identical twin. I think of everything I can about what makes Khalil who he is, while my mouth stays on topic speaking about knives and savagery. I think of how waiters scurry around him, clear tables, fuss, and bring his favorite sweet sage tea. Then, still talking of the murder, I think of how, when he drives through his hometown of Nazareth, drivers honk their horns at Khalil's bus in respect. When I speak about how they took off my Star of David necklace, my mind leaps to jewelry. Khalil's ring. His hands clutch the bed rail, showing off his fake ruby ring, the one that he tells the tourists is genuine. My mind is like Pac-Man, that old computer game, gobbling up thoughts one after another. Pac-Man has a feast.

Without planning or practice, or any conscious control, I glide through the interview. It is like driving along and suddenly realizing that you have traveled miles but have been so deep in thought that not only do you not know how you got there, you are astonished and exhilarated that you have managed to do so without wrecking the car. I can talk about it, without having to think, let alone feel, anything.

Afterwards, when Pasty tells me I was very brave to speak about it, and I was incredibly lucid considering what I had been through, I cannot recall what he meant by "it." So I just give them my best modest smile and say, "You're welcome."

"No, no, it was an accident. I didn't mean to kill anybody."

—Dorothy

CHAPTER 10

Nurse Olga ties a red heart-shaped Get Well Soon balloon onto one of the drips and walks to the table at the end of the room. It is laden with bouquets of roses, carnations, white lilies, wicker baskets of fruits, and parcels of various shapes and sizes wrapped in shiny paper. Above the table is a string pinned to either side of the wall, to which so many cards have been clipped that it sags.

Olga picks up a red package and gives it a little shake. "Ooh, this is from the lady from the British Consulate. I think it's tea. When I told her that you're not a tourist and you don't need to be flown back anywhere, she was so shocked I thought I would have to give her CPR. She had no idea."

She sticks her nose into a bouquet of lilies and sighs.

"Skinny," she says, peeking at the card tied to the stems. "What sort of a name is that? Is that English? You've got about a hundred kisses on it. I kid you not."

I tell her Skinny calls himself that as a form of self-deprecating humor.

"He struggles with his weight. He wears loud T-shirts with slogans like 'I beat anorexia.' You won't believe how he introduced himself to me in tour guide school. After finishing his sandwich, he licked his fingers, shook my hand and ... and ... winked."

Impersonating Skinny, I lick my thumb and wink.

"He likes me but I don't like him, not in that way. We've known each other for years. He is a fantastic photographer. Once he took photos of all the gates of Jerusalem and they were so good he made prints. He sold over a hundred."

Chuckling, Olga comes over and lowers herself slowly and thoughtfully onto the edge of the bed. She tells me she wasn't around for the past couple of days because she was placed in another department. She's sorry about that, but it really was an emergency. The head nurse was sick. At least she was in the right place for that. She is happy the morphine is putting me in good spirits. Do I like my new room? I should. It's so much brighter. It must be so nice to have so many friends drop by. They are such a faithful bunch. I'm a lucky girl, aren't I. I'm quite the celebrity. She watched me on the news. The report was only a couple of minutes, but wow! I was such a rockstar. In all her career, she's never seen so many cards. And to think it's only been a week. Unbelievable, isn't it.

I haven't got a clue. I can't remember being moved to another room, or friends coming by with flowers and cards, or being on the news, or English people bringing me tea.

Blank. It's all a blank. But it's a lovely, empty, blank that makes me feel I am without a care in the world.

Nurse Olga tells me not to worry. What I have been through would make anyone a little forgetful. It could also have something to do with the morphine. Never mind. I must not worry. I wasn't worrying, I tell her, I was only wondering.

She lets out a little chuckle. "Today is a big day, because today you are going to start eating 'proper food.'"

I am no longer relaxed or blank.

"We need to fatten you up," she says. "Plenty of protein drinks will strengthen those old bones of yours. If they're ever going to heal, then you must make sure to drink them three times a day. You have a choice of flavors. Strawberry, vanilla or chocolate?"

Strawberry, vanilla or chocolate? Frankly, I would rather eat my own vomit.

Vanilla it is.

But before Nurse Olga prepares the drink, she has a surprise. She shows me a small flat plastic transparent box divided equally into three vertical compartments. Each compartment contains a ball; red, yellow and blue. Attached to the bottom corner is a crinkled plastic tube, a mini-version of a vacuum cleaner hose. At the end of that is a plastic mouthpiece.

"It's a spirometer," she says cheerfully. "It measures your lung capacity."

According to Nurse Olga, all I have to do is exhale as hard as I can into the tube to make the balls bounce up to some lines along the middle of each compartment. That's all. When I am able to make the balls reach those lines, it's a good sign that I will soon be ready for discharge from the hospital.

Hearing this fills me with hope. I am tired of being on a drip and having bright lights on for most of the day, and hearing other patients cough and spit when my door is open. So I decide to breathe out so hard that not only will the balls reach the lines, they'll pop out of the top and roll all the way across the floor.

The nurse puts the tube in my mouth. "Breathe out hard, sweetie. Breathe out hard."

Giving it my all, I close my eyes and exhale with such force until I see nothing except little white flecks dancing behind my eyelids.

Still blinded, I hear the nurse say, never mind, let's give it another go.

The task is on par with trying to blow up a hot air balloon. No amount of huffing and puffing will make those balls move.

Nurse Olga gives my knee a pat of encouragement. "Let's see if we can get the red one to move. Or would you prefer the blue or yellow?"

I truly don't give a shit what color. I hate every single one. But I can't say that, not because I care about sounding rude, but because I don't have any breath left to talk. I slump against the headboard, head hanging, lungs heaving and saliva dribbling.

The nurse thinks we should try again in a few minutes. I should rest first. In the meantime, she'll go and get my protein drink. Vanilla, wasn't it?

I scowl at those red, yellow and blue little bastards gloating at the bottom of the box. There is not enough time in the world for me to describe how much I loathe them for holding me hostage in the hospital.

Exhausted, I close my eyes, only soon to be disturbed by the clearing of a throat. I hate that sound as much as I hate snorting or slurping. I keep my eyes closed, hoping that whoever it is will go show some sensitivity and not disturb a sleeping and very sick patient.

But it is not to be. I open my eyes.

Agent Oscar.

Not bothering with any formalities, he stuffs his hands in his pockets and takes out a bunch of keys. "They're yours," he says, and grins.

He really is the nicest man. Despite the pressures of his job and being on call night and day, fancy finding my keys and then dropping by to give them back to me. How thoughtful.

"Thank you," I say. "I'm always losing them."

I reach out to take the keys, but he is not having it. He starts to toss them in the palm of his hand. Enjoying the jingle, I follow them with my eyes. Oscar is having fun. With each throw, his eyes widen. The last toss is high. The keys almost hit the lamp hanging from the ceiling. He snatches them up just before they land on the floor.

Oscar's eyes glint with intensity. His voice is rushed, breathless, as if Israel has done the impossible and won the World Cup. "Do you understand, Kay? Think! Your keys were in your bag. Do you realize what this means?"

He grins with his eyes shut.

"We got 'em, Kay. They're in our hands. Kristine's murderers are in our hands."

I barely feel anything, let alone that those who stole her life are "in our hands." All I have is a sensation that Kristine was someone I vaguely knew, probably from childhood. I can't recall what she looked like, where we met, or who she was. Nevertheless, I understand that Oscar and his courageous men have caught a couple of filthy murderers, and this makes for wonderful news.

Oscar and the Shin Bet deserve encouragement, admiration and affection. Unstoppable, I tell them,

"I love you all so much, I wouldn't know which one of you to marry first."

Blood rushes up my neck. My face burns. What an idiotic thing to say! What in God's name was I thinking? I don't know where to look, let alone how to explain. I am so flustered I cannot formulate a sentence.

Oscar is unfazed. He offers me his hand to give him a high-five, which I give him, albeit limply.

"Kay, I told you we would get the bastards, didn't I!"

On his way out, he turns around and tells me to call him if I need anything.

Like change the oil in the car, or pick up some groceries on the way out? As if.

Anyway, I don't even know his real name, let alone have his number.

After Oscar leaves, the implications of who exactly is "in our hands" seep in. It is a sinister, tangible evil. The sensation is suffocating. I feel smothered with fiendish slime. I am gasping, wheezing, breathing my last. I have to get them out of my mind. The only way is to think of something else, to go for the mental "stash."

My brain flees to a scenario in which I travel to Argentina with a briefcase, dark glasses, and a pistol with a silencer. Deep in South American suburbia, I hide in the dark, sweltering behind lampposts, waiting for a couple of oblivious Nazi war criminals to stroll by. I know how to do stealth. Oscar has trained me for months. Timing, distance, speed of walking – I check their every move. All has been surveyed. The plan is flawless. It's time for the mission: to shoot a bullet right between their eyes.

The best part is reporting back to Oscar. I do so at night, under candlelight, from an abandoned building just outside Buenos Aires, the one with a poster of Eva Perón on the window. My only equipment is a transmitter. As it crackles and hisses, I punch out the dashes and dots of Morse code all the way to Jerusalem.

They. Are. In. Our. Hands.

* * *

In comes the Russian doctor with the raccoon eyes. While probing his fingers around my side, he talks to Hannah, who is standing beside the bed with arms folded.

"The lung drain is almost clear," he says. "Her diaphragm is stitched up nicely. The stab wounds are stapled up to perfection and the broken bones will heal in time."

He wants to check to my heart. No doctor has to ask anymore. I know the routine. Unbutton the pajamas and offer my chest to the world. It's available for anyone who wants to have a little look or listen. The doctor circles the stethoscope over my sternum.

He straightens up, digs his chin into his chest, and peers at me over his glasses.

"It's good news," he says, his face one of a man impressed. "Your heartbeat is steady. Your lungs are clear. If it stays like this, we'll take out the drain in a couple of days and you can be discharged."

I eye the depository on the floor. The gunk has diluted in color. No longer raging crimson, it is chewing-gum pink with rust-colored streaks.

Hannah tells him – with a healthy margin of Google-acquired expertise – that two weeks in hospital is not enough.

The doctor looks at her and shrugs. If there was anything more they could do to help, they would. But there isn't anything more they can do. My progress now is down to physical and psychological rehabilitation. Hannah will need to schedule trauma therapy for me, as soon as I am able to stand.

"Besides," he adds, "with the gruel that passes as food here, who in their right mind would want to stay one day longer than absolutely necessary?"

With that, he pulls a pad of stickers out from his coat pocket. Allowing himself a wry smile, he sticks a yellow smiley face on the back of my hand. "Get well soon," it reads in Hebrew.

* * *

After he leaves, Hannah counts on her fingers all the people who have offered to have me stay with them. Over twenty, she tells me, including herself. Options are with various girlfriends, families, couples, singles, tour guides and musicians. Eddie and Orit Klein, old friends, a bubbly couple with an orange grove, are probably the best choice for now, she thinks, because Gedera, the town not far from the coast where they live, is far from the big cities and far from the press. When she says "press," she squeezes my hand. I am not to worry, everything will be fine.

She needs to leave. Without their mother around, her kids think they are in heaven, eating takeout food and watching as much TV as they want. The babysitter is taking liberties. That's her problem and not mine, she says, cheerfully. I don't have to worry about that.

With Hannah gone, I sneak back to Argentina. This time I manage to bump off sixteen Nazis. While replaying this scenario for the seventeenth time, I am interrupted by Ari Davidovitch, who comes in and knocks over the tube of toothpaste on the bedside cabinet with his M16.

The Colonel, as I like to call him, is my friend from guide school, a high-ranking, crack soldier and soft-spoken man. On the rare occasions that he does yell, his voice is legendary. When Ari Davidovitch shouts, he can be heard for miles.

He gives the butt of his rifle a little pat, saying it's far too cumbersome for a place like this, then unslings it and stands it against the foot of the bed.

Brown, bald and with a nose that has been broken countless times, Ari sits down in the plastic chair that has hosted so many others over the last few days. He lifts one foot over his knee and hunches his shoulders until his neck disappears into his furry army-jacket collar. Usually calm, hence also legendary for holding a gun and looking through the sights for up to a minute without blinking an eye, he now fidgets. He switches legs and sways back and forth. I have never seen him like this, let alone seen him sweat. Although he is wrapped up for winter, there are droplets of perspiration under his battle-worn nose.

What on earth is wrong? I should tease him and put him at ease. He likes to tease me, just as I do him. His favorite tease is that I am either a deserter or a coward because I didn't serve in the Israeli army. Whenever he says that, he knows it irritates me. I didn't serve, I always respond, not because I was a deserter, or a coward, but because I was, at twenty, already too old.

"Colonel," I say breezily. "The legendary Israeli army did not need a pale, twenty-year-old asthmatic like me, who scarcely knew any Hebrew then."

He doesn't smile as he always does when I say this. He just sits there, chewing his mouth. Finally, he fumbles in his pants pocket and takes out a phone. He flips it open. Snaps it shut. Flips it open. Snaps it shut. Flip. Snap.

What on earth is wrong?

"There will never be a right moment," he tells me. He holds the phone to his ear. I can just about make out that the ring tone is in E flat.

"Yes, Mr. Luken ... yes ... yes ..."

I am unable to move even a finger, so Ari holds the phone against my ear. Kristine's father sounds so near he could be sitting inside my head.

"Kay ... we've ... we've been trying ever since—"

He stops. For long moments, he just breathes and swallows.

When Mr. Luken speaks again, he does so in a voice so quiet, I can barely hear.

"We just hope the murderers will be caught."

I am not allowed to tell Mr. Luken that the murderers have been captured, but this is not what is on my mind right now. For in this moment of her father's grief, all I want is for Kristine's parents to magically appear beside my bed, so I can fall upon their necks, and hug them tight, and weep, and say I am so, so sorry, and promise them I didn't mean it, and beg for their forgiveness, and plead with them to believe me that it was not my fault, and ... and ... and ...

But my chin is juddering so hard, I cannot make my mouth form any words.

Where I fail to speak, Mr. Luken speaks of love. I must never forget they love me, or that their daughter loved and appreciated me. For the seventeen hours that Kristine was in Israel, they have no doubt it was a happy time.

He seeks to comfort, rather than blame. But instead of salving, his kindness lacerates. I scrunch my eyes and am sucked into darkness. I beg the cosmos for an act of mercy; that every bead of sweat, every drop of blood, every white cell, every red cell, every membrane, every nucleus, and every despicable, slimy, evil, repulsive, nefarious piece of plasma that makes me who I am, will flush through the mattress and evaporate forever.

PART II

"Lions and tiger and bears, oh my!"

—Dorothy

CHAPTER 11

The night I spoke to Kristine's father, everything changed. Until then, I had done all that I could not to think about what had happened, but after that night I could think of nothing else. In the hospital, for the most part, I felt either nothing or at most a mild unease. With a lot of help from the morphine, it was effortless to indulge in fantastical scenarios about bumping off Nazis in Argentina, or floating on the deep blue sea. I sustained no more than a superficial awareness, equivalent to the anxiety induced when needing to pay a fine for a traffic offense. Unpleasant, but-what's-the-point-of-worrying type of attitude.

During the conversation with Kristine's father, an emotional tornado swirled up and thrashed inside, whipping me away. Although this unbridled anguish lasted just moments longer than the conversation itself, the tempest wreaked its havoc. I was left with what I can only describe as internal and external obliteration. Kristine and her world, me and my world, and all that I knew to be me, had been destroyed. And nothing would, or could, ever be the same again.

* * *

In the Indigo Breeze living room of the little house in Gedera with the view leading out to green groves of citrus trees, creepy shadows lurk under the clock on the wall. The hands edge forward, taking me to the hour of the apocalypse, the hour of murky memories scuttling around like rats in the dark. It is the hour where the walls morph into pine forests and canopied skies. The clock ticks and the bells toll; the time of death has come. It is the world of forests, knives and ancient creeds.

Serrated steel obscures the sun, a woman writhes on holy ground, and the next thing I know, I am safe and sound lying on an IKEA futon. In the corner of the room is the television. It is tuned to a radio station and there is a still image on the screen: on one side a map of Israel, and on the other the head and shoulders of a weather forecaster. His frozen face leans into an enormous microphone, as if he is about to eat it. I listen to the weather forecast and stare at him. There will be showers in the north, he says without moving his lips.

Kneeling beside my couch is a thin and delicate woman who looks at me through her little round glasses while rubbing my hand. She looks familiar, but I can't immediately remember her name. I can't remember anyone's name for the first few seconds, anymore. I barely can recall my own. Relief comes when I recall that this is Mira, my very first friend in Israel. But angst returns with vengeance, because now her last name escapes me. These blackouts turn my stomach. What if I am losing my mind? Staring into her eyes, I try to remember. I have a hunch it could be one of those Slavic names with very few vowels, but I'm not sure. It doesn't really matter, I console myself, no one really uses last names in Israel. All that matters is she is here.

"Do you remember when we used to share an apartment in Tel Aviv?" she says. "It was fun, wasn't it?" She keeps rubbing my hand. "Remember how you always used to complain when I left my essays all over the place and pottery shards in the sink? I'm the messy one and everyone thought it was you. I bet you never thought that disarray of papers and books would make you want to be a tour guide."

When I ask her if it's the Sabbath, she looks sad. It's Wednesday, she tells me. Yes, she is sure, because it was Tuesday yesterday. No, it's not four in the afternoon. Really it's Wednesday and really it's only five fifteen in the morning. She closes her eyes and keeps them closed for a long time. I have noticed she does that a lot lately.

"Do you remember that I had to persuade you to do the guide course?" she says, eyes still closed. "You thought you wouldn't pass, and now look at you, there is hardly anything you don't know about Israel." I count the lines on her forehead.

"We have had some fun, haven't we? Do you remember how I would always have to go and get you in from the midday sun in Tel Aviv? You would sit outside the stairwell sweating and smoking a hookah until you couldn't stand the heat any more. That sticky stinky apple tobacco, it always ..." She stops, opens her eyes, and says, "Aww. Peanut licked my finger."

I stroke my dog's ear. Avoiding my left side, she lies on my right because she knows where I hurt. I love how she snuggles. I love my dog. I love everything about her. But Peanut is more than a dog. She is a witness; the only witness.

Since we reunited two weeks ago, she only leaves me to go out to pee. Whichever friend is on duty comes with her beloved leash. But instead of jumping up and down with excitement to go out, as dogs should do, Peanut buries herself under the blanket. They have to lift it off, pick her up and take her out to the orange grove. In peoples' arms her ears go down. She trembles. Often she doesn't make it in time. She leaves a little wet patch on their sleeves.

Mira exudes a weird giggle in which her mouth doesn't even move. "Did I tell you what the paramedic said? He said Peanut was so happy at his house, she thought she was on vacation. See, you had nothing to worry about at all. The dog didn't even miss you."

True to his word, the tousle-haired Magen David Adom paramedic had indeed returned to the forest to rescue my dog. He found her in the dark, shaking under the picnic table. He gathered her in his arms, put her in his ambulance, took her to his home and stitched up her leg.

Mira tickles Peanut's ears. "Go to sleep, Kay," she says. She sniffs and turns her head away.

But I can't sleep. Because if I do, I may see the forest and the fury of men.

Fighting sleep is a war of attrition, not just against exhaustion but against those who bind me up and shove me to my knees. Sleep threatens to put me into a dream in which I relive the eternal hour of four o'clock on that Sabbath afternoon.

Yet there is a dream more terrifying than reliving what happened in the forest. It is the dream I had the other day. It goes like this.

Kristine and I are hiking in a forest when we are attacked by two men. After half an hour, they tie us up, gag us, force us to our knees, then hack at us as if they are chopping down trees. While being beaten and stabbed myself, I watch them fell Kristine. When they leave, I manage to get up and walk until I find help. I am hospitalized and days later I speak to Kristine's father. His voice is broken, he is drenched with grief.

Until that point, the dream is how it really happened. But then it changes.

The hospital and the voice of Kristine's father disappear, and I am at home in Givat Ze'ev being woken up by Mr. Gershoni, my landlord. He is banging on my door, hollering, "Sweetheart, the rent is overdue."

In my dream, I dream that the horror was just a dream.

Then, in reality, I wake up.

At first I'm so relieved to find I am not in a forest that I want to dash through the streets, do a little tap dance and swing around every bottle-green lamppost in Givat Ze'ev, shouting, Thank you, God, it was just a dream!

Then I remember that in Givat Ze'ev I don't have an IKEA futon.

Demons and angels, who oversee our dreams, make me dream it was just a dream. And that is why I am terrified to sleep. To dream it was only a dream is as cruel as the reality itself.

I plunge into *jamais vu*, that horrible opposite to *déjà vu*.

Kristine was murdered. It can't be true. We went for a walk, then she was dead. It can't be true. Kristine was murdered. It can't be true. No matter how much I tell myself it really did happen, I can't make myself really believe it. So I tell myself again.

If time spent on what I think about could be shown on a pie chart, then *jamais vu* would comprise close to one hundred percent. The disbelief of what happened to me and to Kristine is so comprehensive and pervasive that it overlaps, interacts and intersects with most other thoughts.

90

And there are other thoughts. Thoughts of Make-Believe. This is when I construe a new script, with a happy ending, visualizing it all from beginning to end, just like a movie director.

It is the morning of December the 18th. I am at home. Kristine's door is still closed. She is still tired and sleeping after yesterday's flight.

Cue Make-Believe.

I play the piano considerately, so that she can sleep; I keep the soft pedal against the floor and barely touch the keys. When Kristine finally emerges, in this imaginary world, I cook her breakfast rather than handing her a tub of hummus. With her eyes closed she swallows every mouthful and tells me it is delicious. In this happy scenario, as our morning begins, we take as much time as she needs to find as many pottery shards as she wants at Tel Beit Shemesh. We're not in a hurry. I will help her find some ancient jug handles. They will be wonderful gifts for her family. I do everything I can, not only to be her guide, but also to be her friend. All these little thoughtful things I could have done to make her day happier go to make up my world of Make-Believe.

The scene runs forward to that afternoon. Among the pine trees a man pounces on me from behind. I struggle with him on the ground. I manage to twist over, and, seeing my chance, I am empowered with monstrous strength and plunge my penknife right into his heart. He topples back, clutching his chest, trying to stop the gush of blood spurting through his fingers. Follow me, I pant to Kristine. Through the thicket we run for our lives. Kristine's face is flushed, her eyes are bright. She knows I can get us out of danger. We run through the forest until we safely reach the car.

And best of all, in this wonderful world of Make-Believe, Kristine Luken thanks me for saving her life.

Thinking about this happy outcome is like being in a cozy room tucked under a thick feather duvet on a cold Jerusalem night. The room has deep-thread Persian carpets and walnut furniture. On a coffee table is my glass of Chivas Regal, straight, how I like it – never on the rocks. The mellow music of the Oscar Peterson Trio is on and a crackling log fire makes the room warm and orange. That's how good this imaginary scenario feels.

If someone disturbs me while I'm indulging in these happy thoughts, it's as if they have barged into my cozy room, snatched away the duvet

91

and shoved me naked out of the door. The air is biting cold, my breath is blue, my ears tingle and my fingers ache. Frozen and forlorn, I don't know where I am, who I am, or even if I am at all. Although in reality I am on a cotton futon surrounded by friends, I feel entirely alone.

So, shaken from my world of Make-Believe, my thoughts circle back in *jamais vu*.

It just can't be. Kristine Luken is murdered. It just can't be.

The only other reprieve I sometimes have are moments of nothingness, when not even the cries of Kristine Luken are heard, as she is led to her execution. No matter how much I try, and to my great anguish, I cannot create this blissful state of nothingness consciously. It just happens, and all too infrequently. When it does, friends look at me with deep grooves on their foreheads. You asked us the time just minutes ago, they tell me, stroking my hand. We told you what day it is, did you forget?

* * *

Hearing the replay of Kristine's whimpers began the night I spoke to her father in hospital. It came from nowhere and has not left me since. Neither the chatter of my friends, talk radio, a barking dog, a boiling kettle, nor any other noise, mutes this tinnitus of death. For hours on end I swivel my fingers in my ears and try to gouge out her cries. Soon there is a squelch. My ears are warm and wet. When someone pulls out my fingers, they are covered in waxy blood.

For most of the time, I feel as I am listening to life through a stethoscope. Everything is so very loud. Even the dull white noise on a radio that is kept on so unforeseen sounds won't catch me by surprise is not enough to dampen approaching footsteps (Godzilla thrashing down skyscrapers in New York), or heavy breathing (a Negev storm), or the occasional burst of song from birds in the orange grove – which to me is the harbinger of death, as blood-tingling as a barrel of shrieking monkeys. A sneeze, a cough, a squeak, any sudden noise, leaves me so tense that every sinew, ligament and muscle is on the verge of snapping. It is all intolerable, intense, relentless noise.

But, by far the worst, are the whimpers of Kristine Luken.

I hear her cries day and night; and even more so, I see her in my friends who only want to help. Angels no doubt, they are also demons. They become, chillingly, Kristine's doppelgänger. Kristine appears in the way they tie up their hair and how they put on lipstick. She is in the way they put minuscule portions of food on their plates, in their friendly manner, in their thoughtfulness, their devotion and their concern. Then Kristine goes and they are back to being tall or short, fat or thin, dark or light, their always lovely helpful selves.

Team, as I like to call them, have been with me through my stay in the hospital and since my release two weeks ago. Whether it is sitting up, standing, lying down, going to the bathroom, showering, dressing, brushing my teeth, combing my hair, or walking around the living room three times a day (a journey which, by the time I have sat up, done the exercise and sat back down, can take up to half an hour), they are here to help. These people were vigilant when the drip stopped working and blood got into the tube. They were there when the morphine failed. They were there to help me to the toilet. Steadying the lung drain, they tried not to balk at the angry thick crimson swishing in the depository and threatening to spill onto their shoes.

The men in my life are Team as well. Ari, Khalil, Rabbi Feinberg, Skinny, and my fun friend Kenny, who spends half his time sipping rum and sailing the rich around the bays of the Virgin Islands and the other half volunteering in the Israeli army. But it was the women who did and continue to do the up-close and personal care.

For all my friends, the extraordinary has become the ordinary; it is par for the course that I am lying on an IKEA couch with raw flesh, barely able to move. Someone is always on hand to welcome the constant stream of visitors who, undeterred by distance, arrive by plane, bus, train, taxi, car, bicycle or on foot. People come as they are and they come at all times of day and night. No one sleeps, least of all me. It's an open house. People I have never met before come on their lunch breaks, or before work, or after work, or in-between errands. Depending on the changeable winter weather, they arrive sweating or chilled to the bone. They just want to express their condolences. They squeeze my hand and tell me not to give up. They always bring something. It's usually cards, CD's or flowers, along with lots of food, which mostly gives me the adverse and undesired feeling that I am sitting my own *shiva*.

I live with a constant gnawing that the death of Kristine was only the beginning. Death will strike again. Whoever it is, from the moment they leave, I wait for the news they have died. If they come back, all it means is that I know it will happen tomorrow, or the next day, or the next. I know, because outside, the little orange grove is full of life, but inside, death waits to strike.

Faceless, the Angel of Death hovers behind those I love. Oblivious to his presence, they carry on with their everyday chores. A friend moves to the kitchen to make coffee. She reaches for the kettle, but she has not dried her hands. She is about to be electrocuted.

No. Please, no!

She rushes over. Pale and alert she holds my hand. What's wrong, she asks. Was it another flashback? Am I in pain? Do I need water? She makes sure I have everything I need. Now she must go. She will be back in an hour.

She must go.

But if she goes, the Angel of Death will take her. I know she will swerve into an oncoming car. I know she will never return. I hang onto her fingers. Last moments. The only moments she has left. I stare at eyes, gaze at skin, peer at eyebrows and try to store up memories before Death takes them. Please speak. Say something. Anything. Just so I will remember your voice.

It's alright, it's alright, they keep saying, until their voices fade away.

After they make rushed and whispered phone calls, they leave the house accompanied by a faceless hooded creature clutching a scythe.

When I am not thinking of the death of Kristine, or the imminent death of those I love, I think about my own. Death doesn't scare me. It's not like a pair of slimy cold hands intending to throttle me, toss me into a hole in the ground and start shoveling soil. Death has nothing to do with fear or feeling depressed, or being lost in grief. It is just a way out.

As I see it, the hands of Death are manicured and soft. They can lead me to a place where I will not have to think or feel again. For hours, I ponder how peaceful, timeless and cozy it would be to be interred in the earth. The soil around my body would protect me from the noise and endless thoughts and fears. Death is bliss. Death is peace. Death is calm. Death is like floating on the deep blue ocean looking up at white feathery clouds. Yes, Death would be my sea of forgetting, in which there would only be the lull of the waves and no more whimpers of Kristine Luken. Death sounds glorious to me.

Death is everywhere. People are dead tired. They have deadlines. They could murder a steak. They have time to kill. Some visitors have been dying to meet me, although I always thought it was me who had been doing the dying.

Violence too is omnipresent, albeit inadvertently. Israel is full of Six-Day War Streets, Ghetto Uprising Roads, Sinai Campaign Boulevards, Operation This and Operation That, military battles Israelis fought just for the right to exist. There are few Vineyard Avenues, Dandelion Roads or Primrose Drives in Israel and in the neighborhood of my mind.

It is a zeitgeist of death and violence where night and day blur, and there is only pain and endless dark life.

* * *

A three-year-old boy is sitting in front of the television. The volume is low and the child is giggling at a cartoon. A cat chases a mouse around a table with a rolling pin. It catches his prey and bangs the little fellow over the head. A party horn, flattened and rolled into a coil, unravels out of the mouse's mouth and coils in again. In and out, in and out. In this helter-skelter madness, the helpless mouse turns into a puff of smoke and disappears. Forever.

Pummeled. Beaten to death. Butchered. Murdered.

The child points at the television and squeals with delight.

My head is about to explode. My heart is thumping. My chest is tight.

A familiar woman with long blonde hair rushes up to the child. She grabs him and holds him close to her chest. Like a mother bear protecting her cub, she growls at me and walks away. She soon returns to hold my hand and say she is sorry. She didn't mean to snap at me. I try to remember her name.

Even for those I have known, some of them for the last twenty-five years, I have trouble remembering their names. I get confused or muddle them up. That scares me. But everything scares me. They scare me. Noise scares me. Movement scares me. When someone stands behind me, or raises their arm or unties their shoelaces, I clench my fists until my knuckles turn white. Trees, birds and skies, gags, laces and knives, everything scares me. Everything.

During the eleven days I was in the hospital, the pain was mild. When it did come, it felt as if someone was sitting on me, or I was sucking air through a straw, or on occasion, a herd of bison stomping across my chest. Now it's different. With no danger now of pneumonia, lying on a futon in the heart of Gedera, everything is different. Pain is always on. The little pills that brag of killing pain have not wounded or even stunned it. So much for living up to their reputation. The pain is worse than it was in hospital. It is even worse than the actual moments of being stabbed. It is the most painful pain there is.

Think of a paper cut.

Think of a bread knife slicing off the edge off your thumb.

Think of slamming a finger in the door.

Think of crawling on broken glass.

Think of smashing a brick in your face.

Think of banging your bones with a hammer.

Think of sticking pins in your eyeballs.

Think of pulling off your nails.

Now think of all of this happening all at once and accompanying every movement from breathing, yawning, sneezing, swallowing to scratching your nose. Even the *thought* of moving hurts. The pain is never off. The only mild pleasure in this hell occurs when I lift my legs and the sweat-clad cotton falls away, allowing cool air to caress the backs of my knees.

Sitting up is an expedition. It needs preplanning and demands a physical exertion that leaves me more exhausted than climbing Masada, that last bastion of Jewish independence that fell two thousand years ago.

Someone wedges their arms under my armpits and grips their fingers in a vise. Then, inch by inch, they raise me up while someone else slips cushions behind my back, until I am propped up. This is done in slow motion, because I need to breathe and rest in between the inches. From sitting up I am shifted around so my back is against the sofa, and then I am helped to stand up. Standing causes my sweat-drenched pajamas to peel away from my back. When they do, they pull at loose skin. It feels as if a maniac is rubbing me with sandpaper, hoping to scrape me down to the bone. All I can do is bite my sleeve until the cuff is soggy and watch my nostrils flare, unable even to blink away the sweat in my eyes.

Ever since I fell off the toilet seat last week, Team insist that they will wait with me in the bathroom. Still sweating from the pain incurred in standing, arm in arm with Hannah and Mira, or whoever's turn it is, I make another trip. When we shuffle past the kitchen, I catch a whiff of food. Someone is cooking, meals for Team or for the endless visitors. No matter what they're cooking, it always stinks of rotten flesh. But there is an even more sickening smell for me in that magnolia-tiled bathroom – the air freshener, which emanates pine.

While waiting for the inevitable plop, Mira and Hannah chat about a piggish ex and a Second Temple oil lamp recently discovered in the antiquities of the Arbel synagogue, just under a limestone capital on the eastern side. Poop done, they help me up. When they are convinced I am steady, they turn away so I can wipe my butt.

In hospital, I grew used to a half-naked status due to various doctors examining me at all time of day or night. Nudity does not make me naked; helplessness does. It is the same impotence and humiliation I felt in the forest. The vulnerability is so terrifying, and the dependence so shaming, that when people are assisting me, I try to do everything as fast as I can in the deluded hope that no one will notice how powerless I am.

It is about a month after the attack when I first take a look at myself in the mirror. For long moments, I stand in the magnolia-tiled bathroom in Gedera and stare until my eyes sting. That isn't me in the mirror; it is a ghost, an apparition of me. My cheeks are so gaunt that if I lie on my side my face looks as it is about to cave in. Discharge the color of mustard oozes from my puffy lips and my face is covered with hundreds of grazes that look as if they were painted on with a dry brush. My left shoulder is a navy green. It hang an inch lower than the right. My sternum bulges with purple welts. Lancing through the middle of these, in the region of my heart, is a black lesion, over two inches long. And when I turn around, I see that the flesh on my back looks like raw steak.

I no longer recognize myself physically, but neither do I recognize my mind. I cannot sleep, eat, move or hold a basic conversation without help or without forgetting what I am talking about, or to whom I am talking.

I want to remember what I was like before. I want my friends to remember what I was like. But I can't, and my guess is neither can they. What I once was, has been hacked up, chopped and sliced through, and is gone.

"Oh yes. There goes some of me again."

—Scarecrow

CHAPTER 12

After nearly six weeks of a scrupulous and rigid routine of painkillers every few hours, four assisted shuffles around the living room daily (to be executed exactly an hour after the painkillers), and cottage cheese and mashed-up tomatoes administered after a shuffle, breathing is somewhat easier. The sensation that I am sucking air through a straw has gone, thank Heaven. For fear of invoking the stampede on my chest though, I am still cautious about inhaling too deeply. In addition to having to be constantly mindful of every breath, which is truly an exhausting ordeal, another tiresome foe has appeared.

For the last four days and nights, I swear that talons have been clutching the back of my neck. At least, that's what this mother-of-all-headaches feels like. The tautness in my head makes me want to throw up. Whether I am lying down, sitting up, awake or asleep, I wear dark glasses to dull any flicker of light, each of which is a dagger stabbing my eyes. The glasses are new. When Khalil made a special trip all the way to Haifa to bring them, not only did he proudly report back that he got them for free from a man who "owed" him, he also swore they would help. But nothing has managed to dull the pain, not even these oversized, ridiculous ski goggles with their thick velcro straps and rainbow-colored coated lenses.

The easiest solution would be to keep my eyes closed. But I am frightened to drop off and wake up having dreamed it was just a dream. Observing the goings-on around me not only guards me from this hell, it also serves as a mild distraction from the headache. Most of the last few days I have pretended to be asleep, but it's a Catch-22 situation. Although spying keeps my mind in neutral, viewing the ease with which others lead their lives only serves to reflect the intolerable gloom of my own woeful reality.

Orit's husband Eddie, a hulk of a man with beady eyes, spent his morning in the citrus grove and this afternoon has been fixing things in the kitchen. He stoops through the back door to put out the garbage. When he comes back, he forgets to lower his head.

"Ouch," he says rubbing his forehead. "That's probably the thousandth time since we moved here that I've done that. My head is starting to look worse for wear."

He grabs a mug of coffee and waltzes over to me. Do I need anything, he inquiries. By the time I have finished thinking about how good it was that he came over and his frame momentarily obscured the light from the kitchen, it's too late to answer. He has already turned around.

"Great idea, those goggles," he says. "She's out like a light." Then he says that seeing as they are all unexpectedly here, they can talk about things now.

Talk about things? What do they want to talk about? Out like a light? Not a chance. Not me.

Watching, waiting, wondering, I lie completely still. It all sounds so mysterious. What on earth do they want to talk about?

Eddie sits at the head of the table opposite Orit, a slender lady with short hair and a thin face who is partial to dangling earrings and who has made it her business in this grim situation always to wear a smile. Along the side of the table facing me are Mira, The Colonel and Khalil. Sitting with their backs to me are Hannah, Rabbi and Mrs. Feinberg.

Eddie turns to the rabbi. "What do you think, David? Do you have time now?"

The rabbi and his wife (who, with sudden relief, I recall is Molly) nod in unison, like those fuzzy toy dogs with bobble heads that sit on car dashboards. There is no time like the present, they say.

Eddie looks pleased. "I had no idea that you guys were going to drop by today. It's a timesaver."

The soft-spoken Rabbi Feinberg sounds unusually cranky. "In normal circumstances, we would not have driven on the Sabbath. It's only because we felt very strongly that visiting is akin to saving Kay's life that we came today. Judaism commands it. In cases of *pikuach nefesh*, we must break Jewish law."

Eddie is in complete agreement. "David, don't get me wrong. By coming today you have saved her life. She was so down earlier but you perked her up. You know how it is for Kay, even three minutes of conversation is exhausting, yet she was with you all the way."

Molly Feinberg squeezes her husband's hand. "Dear," she says, in a singsong voice. "It wasn't a criticism about driving on the Sabbath. Eddie is just saying that because we're already here, we might as well stay a little later for a chat."

In the moments of silence that follow, I study Mrs. Feinberg's hair, which rests on her shoulders and curls inwards at the ends, recalling that Khalil once told me that the great benefit of *sheitels,* the wigs worn by religious women, is that even women in their late fifties can look twenty years younger.

To Khalil's visible disappointment, Eddie announces that courtesy of Molly Feinberg, today is vegan. Eddie smiles across at his wife and asks her to pass the beets.

Mira is taking me to my first session of trauma therapy tomorrow, he informs everyone. On Monday, he and Orit have a meeting with the council about the water pipe, and on Tuesday Hannah has a school play.

Eddie stretches across the table to take a bowl of asparagus. "We are very happy to have Kay here. As far as we're concerned, she can stay forever. However, we know getting here is tricky. This place is out of the way. It's better for Kay and her friends if she could stay with someone more central."

Orit brings bad tidings with a smile.

"Unfortunately, Mick and Miriam still haven't found a suitable place."

The Colonel looks up. "Nothing at all?" A small piece of vagrant lettuce dangles from his mouth. "I thought they had found something in Modi'in."

"There is something suitable, but it's not available until March."

The Colonel frowns. "That's nearly two months away. Why is it so hard to find somewhere in Modi'in? What sort of place are they looking for?"

He gestures for the beets.

Hannah hands him the bowl. "Something long-term," she says. "A place where she can have her own en suite bathroom and a separate outdoor entrance. If and when she needs company, people will be around, but at least she can have her privacy too. Do you want some vinaigrette with those beets, Ari?"

No thank you, The Colonel tells her. Too much acid of late doesn't agree with his digestive system.

He wants to know how are Mick and Miriam going to afford it. "He works in Holy Bagel. It's not going to be easy."

"They're not fazed," says Hannah. "They want to do it and Kay wants it too. When they told her the other day, it was the first time that I've seen so much as a flicker of a smile cross her face since the attack."

The rabbi fiddles with his Beit Shemesh Blue Sox yarmulke. He thinks two months shouldn't be a problem. They could divide the time among them all.

"We could certainly have her at our place for a couple of weeks."

"Us too," says Ari. "Kay staying with us at the kibbutz wouldn't be an issue at all."

Hannah is happy to host me as well.

Eddie looks at her long and hard. "Hannah, it will be an enormous stress for you. Don't take it personally, but you don't look great. You've lost a lot of weight."

Everyone chimes in. Hannah is much too thin. How much weight has she lost? There won't be anything left of her soon. She should eat more.

Orit slips a bowl of greens next to Hannah's plate. "Is Kay really in the frame of mind to be around a household with children, Hannah? Not your children per se, but any kids?"

Hannah is defiant. "She is my friend. If I want Kay to stay at my place, then that is what I'll do."

Eddie is not having it. "For six weeks you've run back and forth like a chicken without a head, and that's in between being a single mother and having a full-time job. There are other solutions for now."

"I think my husband is right," says Orit. "Remember the other day. It wasn't easy, was it?"

Hannah obstinately clutches her fork. "I couldn't get a babysitter for Gideon," she says. "That's all. Their father refused to take him."

The Colonel wants to know what happened.

"I had to bring Gideon here, so I stuck him in front of the television. The cartoons were on. God knows what went on in Kay's head. She snapped. 'What's wrong with that effing cat?' she said. 'He's murdering the mouse!'"

Khalil is wide-eyed. "She actually said 'effing?'"

"Not exactly," says Hannah, coyly. "She said 'fucking.'"

The Colonel shakes his head. "Don't we all?" he says.

"It's not that, Ari," says Hannah. "I try not to swear around the kids, so I'm sure Gideon didn't even understand what Kay said. It was the tone in her voice. She seethed. She was ready to kill. It terrified him."

The Colonel puffs out his cheeks. "That's post-traumatic stress disorder for you. I know it from my soldiers. They withdraw into their shells, never talk about anything, then suddenly, it's like a bomb going off. They blow up over the smallest things, if you'll pardon the pun."

Mira looks at Hannah. "Was Gideon alright?" she asks, softly.

"I think so, but I couldn't … I couldn't help it. I just … I just …"

"Couldn't what?"

Orit pokes a napkin into Hannah's white-knuckled fist. "Don't worry, dear. It's a mother's instinct. You shouldn't feel bad. I would have snapped too. How old is Gideon now? Is he three yet?"

Hannah nods. Yes, Gideon is three, he just turned three. Everyone gives a little, "Aww, how cute," because Gideon has just turned three. Orit spoons heaps of greens onto Hannah's plate.

"Eat please, dear. You're far too thin."

The irony of fattening Hannah up with lettuce is not lost on Khalil, who in a polite yet nonchalant voice comments that there is always a place in life for meat. His remark is met with a chilly silence overridden by the clinking of cutlery.

Eddie wants to keep on point, wrap stuff up. David and Molly have a long drive back.

"David, here's where we need your help. You know Kay's landlord well. She needs to terminate the contract as soon as she can. Trouble is, for him it's not an easy place to rent out, and for her, she doesn't have the money to throw away and frankly nor do any of us. Do you think you can speak to him?"

"What, David?" says Orit. "Why are you smiling?"

The rabbi puts his arm around his wife. With a good deal of satisfaction, he tells them that he and Molly have already spoken to Mr. Gershoni.

He gives her shoulder a little rub. "We saw it coming, didn't we, dear?"

Molly says that Mr. Gershoni was terribly upset about the attack. He sat on the sofa with his head in his hands. When he finally looked up, his face was bright red. His wife had to tell him to lie down because of his blood pressure. They said that if they were more stable financially, they would let Kay have the place for free. Khalil thinks it is very generous of Mr. Gershoni to agree to terminate the contract at short notice. That kind of stuff doesn't happen a lot where he lives. Every woman stays with her parents until she is married. It protects them. They don't have to pay rent. He still doesn't know why Kay turned down his offer to come and live with them a few years ago.

"I had a peek inside Kay's house," says Molly. "She doesn't have a lot of stuff. Kitchen chairs, coffee table, microwave, sofa, bed, fridge, about five hundred books and a set of Encyclopedia Judaica. We could all take something and store it. It's hardly a household."

"You forget the piano," says Hannah.

"The piano? No, dear, I didn't forget the piano. There is simply no solution at the moment, that's why I didn't mention it. There is nowhere to put it and moving it would damage it."

Hannah's voice is terse. "Are you saying we leave it there and sell it to Mr. Gershoni? Kay would be devastated. Anyway, what would he do with it, the man is deaf!"

"Of course I wasn't suggesting that, dear. I wouldn't dream of such a thing. I was trying to explain, that's all. Have you got any ideas?"

Hannah snaps. "Pay for storage. Loan it out. Put it under the kitchen sink. Make a plan."

Forks and knives tinkle on plates. Molly Feinberg quietly asks Mira to pass the kale. Please. Mira passes the kale. It is in a bowl painted with yellow and orange daisies. Mira says it's a beautiful bowl. Orit says thank you dear, it was a wedding present. The whole set is over there in the dining room cabinet. That was a wedding present too. Mira says it's a beautiful set. Orit says thank you again. Mira says you're welcome.

The conversation continues with stops and starts. Because Mira's father is in hospital (although Molly Feinberg notes that he is in marvelous shape for eighty) it is decided that after Mira has brought me back from trauma therapy tomorrow, she will take a couple of days off. With plenty of help on hand, there's no need for Mira to overdo things.

Eddie reads out the schedule. Stephanie, Tami, Gila and Orit will share shifts. Tzvika called late last night to say his wife, Dafna, has a doctor's appointment. She can't miss it. He knows that she would, but he told her she can't. Not this time. She already canceled an earlier appointment to be here last week. She'll come on Thursday instead. It's better that way. She can come with Gila, who also lives in Jerusalem, and they can pick up Linda too. That leaves Wednesday open.

Orit can take the day off on Wednesday.

"That's insane," says Eddie, crushing a napkin in his fist. "You've already taken too much time off."

"I'm sorry," says Orit. "Kay's health is more important than work."

"That's not what I'm saying, Orit. You know I love having Kay here. But if you lose your job we will not be able to help at all and considering that we have a whole list of people on this standby list that would be a very stupid thing to do."

Food in pretty bowls is politely passed around the table.

Molly Feinberg finally breaks the silence. "It's been a long six weeks. Jaded nerves, long nights, we all need a good cry."

A good cry? None of them has ever said they need a good cry. These people have been like parents to a child, invincible and faultless adults, eternally strong and always there. They loved helping. Everything was going to be fine. I am progressing wonderfully, they like to say. But now, they are tired of me.

The Colonel clears his throat. "This is very difficult for everyone. No one is equipped for it. It is stretching us all. How many flashbacks has it been today already, for God's sake? Thirty?"

"Thirty-seven," says Hannah.

"Thirty-eight actually," chimes Mira. "She had one when you were out with Peanut."

The Colonel says many of his soldiers have flashbacks. He has a bit of experience with PTSD. It's terrifying. Maybe he can help.

"It's not just the flashbacks that are scary," Mira says. "It's that look."

"What look?"

"The one where she stares at the clock. It's like she's stuck in time. Sometimes I think she's in a coma. I don't know that I can even impersonate it. It's something like this. It's like her eyes are those of a dying animal."

Ari Davidovitch puts his hand on his chest as if he is in pain. What triggers it, he asks.

"Everything," she says.

"Be specific."

"Well, once there was that stupid commercial on the TV. Do you know which one I mean? The one about car insurance, where three men are all giggling and—"

"I know the one," says The Colonel. "That company's a rip off. It took them eleven months to process a claim of a meager two thousand shekels. My wife was furious. It wasn't even her fault."

Khalil reaches into his pocket. "I have a cousin who works in insurance, Ari. Let me give you his number."

The Colonel holds up his hand. "I'll get it later, my friend," he says. "Thanks though. Go on, Mira."

"Well, I can hardly believe I'm saying this, but I forgot that in that commercial after the music, those guys start joking around. I don't know what I was thinking. Arabic never crossed my mind."

Eyes turn to Khalil. He shrugs a long and high-shouldered shrug that pushes his brown flabby neck over his cream collar. He loves Jews, he tells everyone, and he is as Israeli as everyone else, but he really does think Jews should make more of an effort to learn Arabic. Could he have some more asparagus, please.

"You're right," says The Colonel with a manly guffaw. "Apart from the rabbi, you're the most devout Jew here. Did you guys see that ring he bought for Kay? It has 'Shema Yisrael' on it!"

Khalil has a twinkle in his eye. Would the good lady please pass him the artichoke. Molly Feinberg hands him the bowl. Their health has improved tremendously since they went vegan, she says. They have so much more energy, and they've lost a lot of weight. Her blood pressure is down. Has Khalil ever thought of going vegan?

"Let's stay on point," says The Colonel. "Khalil doesn't need to eat vegan."

Hannah has printed out new instructions. It's a mystery where the old list went. It was always next to the Chinese menu on the fridge. She has a copy for everyone. It is agreed by all that Hannah is very thoughtful, always one step ahead.

The Colonel reads out the instructions. "Painkillers every four hours. An hour after painkillers one lap around the living room. Cottage cheese and tomatoes after exercise." He looks up.

"Why is 'never, ever stand behind her' underlined with three exclamation marks after it?"

"Oh that," sighs Hannah. "Poor Kenny. He flew in especially from the Virgin Islands. He could only come for five days. What a lovely man. He brought a bottle of Chivas Regal, and an old road sign saying 'Beware of the Mines.' I think it was from the Golan Heights. She likes that sort of stuff. Anyway, he wanted to surprise Kay with his visit, but he made the mistake of creeping up behind her. It was such a shame. It took her days to calm down."

Orit says that after that incident, Eddie moved the futon against the wall. "It avoids any possibility of someone coming up behind her again. It works well beside the wall, don't you think?"

Heads turn. Oh, shit! Maybe they saw that I'm awake. Hardly breathing and eyes snapped shut, I listen.

—It looks nicer there. It certainly gives a bit more space than in the middle of the room.

—Yes. Much better. Not too big and clumsy, and as you say, makes a good amount of room for the visitors.

—We took that picture down, didn't we, darling. The one of the Jerusalem Mountains. Trees. You know how it is with trees. Not good for Kay at all. It's really all a learning experience.

—Have you noticed how clingy she is?

Clingy? They think I am clingy. How humiliating!

—Clingy? What do you mean?

—Well, the other day, I had to pop out for an hour. When I went up to her to say see you later, she grabbed my arm. I had to pry myself away, and all the while she kept saying, please don't go, please don't go. It's not like nobody else was here.

—She does that to me too.

—And me. She does it whenever anyone is about to leave. She hangs onto them like they are going to die.

—Ari, have you heard anything under the radar about the investigation?

—Not yet. Give it time. They are clearly working on catching a whole cell. Six weeks is nothing when it comes to catching terrorist cells.

—At least the media are behaving themselves now, after not getting her name right. Fancy calling her Susan. Kay would die if she knew.

—Susan. Oh my God, that's so not Kay.

—And a tourist too. That's even worse than Susan. She prides herself on being Israeli.

My skin is crawling. They think I am clingy, and the Israeli public thinks I am a tourist called Susan. I wish I could melt into the futon and never be seen or heard of again.

"Follow the Yellow Brick Road."

—Glinda, the Good Witch of the North

CHAPTER 13

Down the end of a long gray corridor on the seventh floor of Hadassah Ein Kerem Hospital is a door with a picture of a flower, the kind four-year-olds draw to make their mothers proud. The petals are colored with crayons that stray rebelliously over the lines. The center is a face with goggling eyes and a mouth like a banana. Above this masterpiece, scribbled in Hebrew and Arabic is, "Welcome to Hadassah Ein Kerem Mental Health Clinic."

Mental.

Why the hell does it have to say "Mental?" Why can't it just say Therapy Room or Counseling Clinic? And why does it have to be written in letters so damn huge that people on the other side of Jerusalem can see me go in?

With a buzz the door opens. A nurse steers my wheelchair – a necessary form of transportation to tackle the endless corridors – to a fluorescent space with white walls decorated with photos of oceans, deserts and sunsets. Reception is at the end of the room. With its sliding glass windows it looks like a ticket booth. Waiting beside it is a tufty-haired man in a jogging suit and furry slippers. A scrawny woman with a hedgehog haircut strokes his shoulder. This prompts him to make a noise like he is slurping soup – a sound I particularly loathe.

A copy of *National Geographic* lands on my lap.

My nurse informs me that I love animals. As if to prove it, she flips through the journal and shows me a photo of a baby baboon. With one hand, the primate swings from a tree, with the other, he picks at his genitals.

"Isn't nature wonderful," she says.

A young woman with no make-up and a shoulder-length auburn *sheitel* approaches me. She offers me her hand. Her skin is milky white and her nails are unpolished. A gold band is on her finger.

"I'm Dr. Rozenberg," she says. "Let me show you through." She hands the monkey magazine to the nurse and takes the wheelchair and pushes me into a small room with a desk, a couple of chairs and a geranium.

She turns me around to face her. Religious, married and not looking a day over twenty-five, the person who has been charged with the task of saving me from insanity is sitting three feet away, on the other side of the world.

Dr. Rozenberg tugs her skirt over stockinged knees. She brushes her lap while smiling at me, so I look above her at a poster on the wall. It is of a young couple with matching white shirts, white teeth and spotless skin, smiling happily at all who come through the doors of therapy. At the top in a Hebrew font, the kind inscribed on ancient scrolls, is "Premium Health Insurance."

"Therapy," Dr. Rozenberg says, "is a process. It will give you tools to cope. It is usually no longer than four months, one session a week. This is followed by one session a month for the rest of the year. Having a starting and finishing point is something that most people find helpful. Though if you feel it is inadequate, there can be more."

Dr. Rozenberg hopes this resonates with me.

Nothing about this resonates with me. Nothing at all. I should be out guiding tourists or walking my dog, or in a jazz club just living my life.

To start with, she explains, I need to fill out a questionnaire.

"On the form are two columns. One contains a statement that describes a mood or feeling, the other column is left empty for you to grade yourself with a number. A one means you strongly disagree. A seven means you strongly agree. You can grade yourself anywhere in between. There are no right or wrong answers."

A summary of mental illness.

Even my handwriting will doom me with a verdict of sick. "Untidy" means I am depressed. "Neat" shows I have OCD. "Inconsistent" means schizophrenia and "correct" reveals a deep-seated psychopathic need for control. Whatever way I fill it out, it means that, hours from now, I will be an incarcerated medicated zombie condemned to spend the rest of my days with those who doodle crayon flowers. I look towards the window. On the sill, the pink potted plant lurches for freedom towards the sun.

"If you lock me up, I will kill myself."

Dr. Rozenberg scratches her head. Her *sheitel* shifts ever-so slightly.

"Lock you up? I cannot think of a more inappropriate solution than locking you up. Besides, the Outpatient Clinic does not have the facilities. What were you thinking?"

My cheeks flush. Whipping through the questions, I mutter under my breath, "Thank you, God, thank you, thank you, that I am not going to be institutionalized."

—I am a failure.

—I am uneasy around those I do not know.

—People do not know my dark secrets.

—You never know when something bad will happen.

—Someone else would not have gotten into that situation.

—I feel as if the same event could happen again.

—I try to do what I can in order not to think about what happened.

—I have difficulty sleeping.

—I can never again return to the site where it took place.

Truth be told, therapy is easier than I thought. I will soon be out of here.

—I feel irritable.

—I feel as if I need to wake up because it is just a dream.

—I cannot connect with people around.

—My friends and family do not understand me.

—I sometimes cannot remember the names of my loved ones.

—I have unwanted memories of the event.

—The traumatic event happened because of my behavior.

—I do not know where time goes.

—I have thoughts of suicide.

—I feel dead inside.

Seven.

Every. Single. One.

I look at my watch. It has been five weeks, three days and nineteen hours since the attack. It took only three minutes to fill out the form. Three minutes, once a week, for sixteen more weeks, is a total of forty-eight minutes. Over the course of the next four months, all I have to do is fill out a questionnaire every week and the whole process will take a total of just forty-eight minutes. Then I will be free.

I pass her the clipboard.

"That was quick," she says, pleasantly.

I smile my best cooperative smile, thinking only of the glorious moment when therapy will all be over.

Dr. Rozenberg sits in silence, going over my answers and making notes with her scratchy pen. Her face is expressionless. She gives nothing away.

Finally, she asks, "Are you self-medicating?"

During the course of Kenny's short visit, I was always glad to have a shot of his Chivas Regal from Duty Free. Surreptitiously we drank from coffee cups. Mixed with a sleeping pill, it proved effective for an hour or two. A little woozy, and in sincere appreciation, I blithely promised Kenny marriage under Israel's sunset. He quoted Frank Sinatra. Anything to get me through the night, whether it be prayer, tranquilizers or a bottle of Scotch.

Dr. Rozenberg is waving her hand in front of my face. "Are you self-medicating?"

"Only through prayer," I say.

She seems pleased; maybe she thinks I have hopped on to the religious train.

"I'm not here to judge you, she says, all smiley. "Drink and drugs numb people so they don't need to deal with overwhelming emotions. It's just a natural way of coping. Therapy will help you face your feelings in a much better way."

Am I able to concentrate for a couple of minutes, she wants to know. She wants to explain a few things.

"Unsurprisingly, you have severe PTSD. I want to run through what that means, to put your mind at rest."

She shows me a sheet of paper. It depicts three overlapping circles with words inside: avoidance, detachment, hyper-vigilance, blackouts, numbness, mood swings, flashbacks, nightmares, rage, self-hatred.

"Trauma works like this," she says, pointing to the circles. "Unlike regular memories, our minds are unable to process traumatic ones. Because we feel like the event may pop up randomly and frequently at unwanted and unexpected times, we train our minds to wander. You may catch yourself daydreaming, counting, humming, or developing a fascination with any little detail.

"Traumatized people are afraid that if they don't keep busy by thinking of everything-else-but, the trauma will return. It's compulsive. It's called avoidance. Avoidance is not wanting to think about it, because we dare not think about it."

She points to the section that says "avoidance." Then, pointing to another part, she says out-of-body experiences are also common with severely traumatized people like me.

"It's a subconscious reaction that enables people to see the event as non-threatening because they can look at the trauma from a distance, rather than live through it. Think about it. If there is no way out and you have to talk about it, your psyche, that is the part of you that knows what happened, is left with no other option, except to go upwards and beyond."

Apparently, not only do traumatized people like me not dare to think, they also do not dare to feel.

"That's why you feel dead inside," she says. "Avoidance, detachment, feeling numb, all these things are self-protection."

Listening to the doctor does bring me a little hope, not that I will ever be able to deal with this monster or put my life back together, but because I begin to realize that this information would not exist if I was the only one to whom trauma had happened. Maybe I am not entirely alone.

The doctor says that over the next few months we will work hard. "It's not going to be easy, and you will feel worse before you feel better, but eventually you will feel an improvement. This week, I want you to make an 'avoidance list,' anything that reminds you of the event, things that you don't want to think about or be around, things that you don't want to do. But for now, please, could you just take a couple of minutes to tell me what happened in the forest."

I let my eyes wander to the old wooden table legs, across the mottled tiles and down to her shoes. They remind me of the shoes worn by Israel's first and only woman prime minister, Golda Meir. Frumpy sensible shoes with square heels and not even a touch of style. Dr. Rozenberg pivots the balls of her feet then puts her heels back on the floor. She moves her toes. It looks as if her feet are about to hatch. Who knows, maybe there will be ten little baby Dr. Rozenbergs poking their heads out in another eight months and they will all be wearing wigs.

"Kay, are you with me?"

I look up. She asks if I can think back to that afternoon.

"I can't," I say.

She nods slowly. "I understand," she says softly. "Let's think through this together so you don't feel this is useless. You were scared and I suspect you were many things at once. You were confused and shocked. You felt responsible for protecting Kristine and my guess is that at times you were sometimes probably feeling overjoyed because you thought they were going to let you go."

I narrow my eyes. How does she know what happened? I didn't tell her. She must have seen me on the news. Oh my God, if she read the papers she thinks I'm a tourist called Susan. She doesn't trust me. She thinks I murdered Kristine! A flush crawls up my face and culminates with a tickle of perspiration under my nose.

"I didn't do it," I say, to the lonely geranium that blushes and hangs its head in shame.

Dr. Rozenberg asks me to look at her. "What didn't you do, Kay?"

"I didn't murder Kristine."

Deep in thought, she twists her mouth.

She asks me to try to listen. "Survivor's guilt fills a person with self-hatred. It's like we are fishing, hoping for a bite that will confirm that we are not wanted, or are disgusting or to blame. When you're traumatized, the world becomes unsafe and hostile. Even one word is enough to send us spiraling into self-hatred and suicidal thoughts. That's what trauma does. Does that make sense?"

Technically it does, but how to move information from my head to my heart is a different matter. It is not going to happen. Ever.

"Yes," I say through my teeth.

"There is a lot of hope," she says. "Feeling safe is the beginning. That's what therapy is for. Therapy allows you to say things that you cannot say to anyone else, especially those closest to you."

I watch her get up to go to the window. She opens the blinds. Outside is a building site. I don't look at her when she is talking. Instead I look at a dusty truck rolling over steamy black asphalt. While watching the wiggly waves of heat rise from the tarmac, I think of Hannah. This morning she came early again before turning around to travel back thirty miles to rush the kids to school and start work at eight. Hannah, who is usually as cheerful as a breezy bottle of summer Chardonnay, bright, fun and with plenty of flair, was flat as uncorked Champagne. Her once full cheeks were pale and sunken, and very unusual for Hannah, who used to look good even when she took out the trash, she hadn't even brushed her hair. When she told me she had a medical form for me to fill in, she didn't look me in the eye. She always looks me in the eye. Why didn't she look at me? I know why. She knows what a bad person I am. She hates me and just didn't want to say.

I'd think, now that Dr. Rozenberg is speaking about the effect on others, that I would be mindful also of their struggles and sacrifices to make my life better. But I am not, because I have convinced myself that people are only saying nice things for the sake of saying them.

I don't think of the effect my PTSD has on all those others who have selflessly helped me. I think only of me.

Me, glorious me.

Oh, my God, they said I was clingy. How could they say I was clingy? I didn't ask for my life to be destroyed. It just happened. I wish I had their petty little lives. I wish I could complain about paying too much for insurance, or the vinaigrette being too lemony, or being half an hour late home. For fuck's sake, I don't even have a home anymore and the whole country thinks I am a tourist called Susan who murdered her friend.

I hear the doctor say my name, and that therapy is safe, and that although it feels scary, it's normal that it would arouse some anger.

"Angry?" I hiss. "I'm not angry."

She crosses her knees and gives her skirt another little brush. "It's hard to identify anger, because fear often covers it up. Think about it. We get angry because we are scared of losing control. There is fear of losing those you love because they do not understand you. You fear they will reject you. It's easier to sabotage relationships because it's self-confirming. It is also less painful than facing the possibility that there will be those who for their own valid reasons and limitations cannot take the stress of your new situation and will need to pull away. There is the fear of losing these relationships, the fear of the present, the fear of the past, the fear of the future, and just even one of those fears is enough to make a saint rage."

"Rage?" Spit shoots through my teeth. "I'm not raging! I'm just a little irritable."

She gives me a look of understanding and acceptance and tells me that we will deal with one thing at a time. Then she lays out the plan.

"There are three sorts of therapy that will be done consecutively. Firstly, there is something called Cognitive Behavior Therapy."

She starts talking about me building a fence and the wind blows it down. I tell her I would never build a fence and I don't even know how to hammer a nail into the wall. It's just an example, she says, with a tight little smile. You build a fence, it gets blown down. What would be your first reaction? Would you blame the wind, or blame yourself for not making it strong enough? Would you tell yourself that you're better at some things than others, or would you call yourself an incompetent idiot, bad at everything, and say the fence is just an example of what a terrible person you are.

"I would say I'm an incompetent idiot, bad at everything, and the fence is just an example of what a terrible person I am."

The doctor says that Cognitive Behavior Therapy will help me understand that my thoughts determine my feelings and not the other way around. Feelings come second. It is thoughts that are crucial in the process of healing. I have to use my brain.

Weighing this up, I think this amounts to nothing more than a fruitless exercise in make-believe. The only advantage may be to look on the positive side, to see the glass as half full. Pretending that I like myself, instead of telling her that I watched Kristine die to save my life, is probably better than being in a mental institution, held down on a steel table by burly Russian doctors with a leather strap over my forehead and a cotton wad to bite on while they administer electric shocks.

Dr. Rozenberg says that another part of treatment is Gradual Exposure Therapy. What is the worst scenario you can think of, she asks, the last thing in the world that you would want to do?

I narrow my eyes. "I am not going back there. Let me repeat myself, just in case you don't understand. I am not in a million years, ever, going back to that forest, or to any other forest for that matter. Ever."

As if she hasn't heard me, she says we will start with just a couple of trees. She doesn't mean the trees in the Matta Forest, but other trees. Are there any trees where I'm staying. An orange grove? How lovely. No, she is not suggesting I go alone, I should take a friend. Yes, if I insist, for this first time, he or she can be armed, but the goal is to be near a couple of trees without having that sort of protection. What I have to do is look at a tree or two for one minute, just one minute, note my heart rate and other sensations, then when that is done come back inside. Just one minute, that's all. Too much? Yes, yes, of course she understands. It's not a problem. Let's try for ten seconds instead.

We compromise on five. Five seconds this week, six the next, and so on.

121

The third part of therapy is writing. I must recount the event as vividly as possible without leaving out any of the details. This means that over the coming weeks I will have to think not just about what happened chronologically on that day, but to become aware of each moment; what I saw, heard, tasted, smelled and touched.

My God. I might as well be back in the forest on my hands and knees!

"Yes, I know you don't want to, Kay, but if you don't do this, your mental state will deteriorate. PTSD, when not treated, has a horrible effect on you and, remember, upon those who care for you. It can be devastating for everyone. I want the best for those who care for you, but more than anything I want the best for you."

Care for me? My ass! Dr. Rozenberg is doing this only because she gets paid for it. Just like all that talk I heard from my so-called friends last night with their bullshit care. They think I am clingy. If I was wearing them out then they should have said so, instead of looking for a way to pass me around like a used pair of shoes. And now, to add insult to injury, here is this Dr. Rozenberg, who is too young to have seen anything of life, giving me advice and pretending she cares. No one cares, no one at all. How could I have let myself believe they did? What an idiot. Not only am I an idiot, I am a clingy, stupid idiot.

I look up at the poster behind her. The perfect couple gloat down at me with their perfect teeth, perfect skin and perfect fucking lives. I imagine their skin peeling off and their teeth falling out.

It feels good.

"Who me? I'm not a witch at all, I'm Dorothy Gale from Kansas."

—Dorothy

CHAPTER 14

This ride from trauma therapy at Hadassah Hospital to the Jaffa Gate police station should have taken 20 minutes, at most. This is where, I was told by a social worker who came to see me yesterday, I need to pick up a Victim of Hostilities form issued by the Ministry of Defense so that I can start the endless task of battling the infamously obtuse bureaucracy involved in obtaining some measly monthly pension to help me pay the rent.

But the 20-minute detour has so far turned into an hour and forty-five minutes of claustrophobic, smoldering hell.

I am seated in the back of Mira's car, which is stuck in traffic at the junction that leads up to Jaffa Gate of the Old City of Jerusalem. Coughing exhausts and revving engines make up the din. Bumper-to-bumper, vehicles stretch three hundred feet in front of us and a good half a mile behind. If I had the strength, I would get out of the car and throttle every driver with my bare hands. That would make them shut up.

To our right towers the Citadel of David, to our left is nothing but traffic and up ahead is an impromptu sign hanging from the stop light. "No access to private vehicles," it reads. Not "Sorry for the inconvenience," or any helpful hints pointing towards an alternative route, just "No access to private vehicles."

Typical, thoughtless, rude, short-sighted, irritating Israel.

Mira honks her horn for the tenth time in as many seconds. "It's worse than the Exodus from Egypt," she says, and puffs out her cheeks.

With the right lane now accessible only to taxis, cars are trying to squeeze into the left lane. The traffic has almost ground to a halt. Mira says there is no other option. She will have to put me in a taxi here while she goes and parks the car. She doesn't care if it's a private taxi with a passenger already in it. This is an emergency. I can barely walk, let alone three hundred feet up a hill. She will explain to the driver I am not feeling well.

Ignoring Mira, I stare out of the window at a group of people with red caps standing on the slope below the Citadel. They huddle around a woman in a wide-brimmed hat who is pointing out this and that. The tour guide and her group ushers in memories of my disappeared world.

Through the rearview mirror, Mira looks at me with anxious eyes. "When you feel up to it you can give me a tour. I've not been there for a while, and I would love to go."

I don't say anything. Instead, I look down at my feet, hating my new sneakers. These shoes have no hope of my ever breaking them in by walking the land; they serve only to stomp on any dreams I may harbor of returning to the job I love. I hate these shoes. I hate this traffic. I hate this noise. I hate it all.

"Here's a taxi," says Mira, with excitement. "Here's a taxi, here's a taxi!"

"I need a *sherut*," I growl, looking for one of Israel's minivan taxis. "Not a taxi. There's far more room in a *sherut*."

Two out of the three seats available for passengers are already taken in this taxi that Mira has spotted. I do not want to be crammed in.

"I can't do it," I say. "There's only one space in the back."

Mira raises her eyebrows. "It's not ideal. But there is not a *sherut* in sight. You can't walk up the hill. You can't even walk to the bathroom. This is as good as it's going to get."

She pumps the horn to get the taxi driver's attention and rolls down the window.

"This is an emergency," she says. "It's your chance to do a good deed."

126

Using the old Ottoman name for the police station, she asks him how much he wants to the *Kishleh*. He could even do it for free, she suggests. It's on his way anyway. It's just up the hill.

Unfazed, the bald-headed driver stubbornly raises four fingers.

Mira's voice rises in disgust. "Forty shekels to the *Kishleh*? You have to pass by there anyway!"

He stares ahead and fiddles with the furry Maccabi Tel Aviv dice hanging from his rearview mirror. Mira begs him again. He nods at the three improvised lanes of taxis that are nudging and squeezing their way up towards the ancient breached gate.

Forty shekels it will have to be.

With Mira's help, and with pain raging through bones I didn't even know I have, I edge myself into the back seat, to the accompaniment of irate car horns. Quoting some Bible verse about exploiting the needy, the sick and the homeless, Mira slaps the money into the driver's hand. He says something about having a wife and nine kids to support. Mira retorts, "Don't we all," and tells me I am to wait on the steps of the Citadel while she goes to park. The driver rolls up his window, cutting off Mira's words. I think she is saying she will be as quick as she can.

Inside this Dante's inferno of a taxi, the air is choked with the stink of smoke-stained car seats, human sweat and cheap perfume. Next to me is a pair of thighs. Not just any old thighs, but occupying thighs, fat thighs, thighs covered in a dress with a faded pattern of sunflowers. These thighs are taking up two-thirds of the entire back seat. Their owner is a middle-aged woman with a sweaty pudgy nose and dyed-orange curly hair.

There is a general unspoken guideline in Israel that the more clothes people have on, the more religious they are, and vice versa. Given that yardstick, this lady, with her bare, flabby arms and low-necked, speckled-with-sweat generous cleavage, could be commanding a secular revolution.

For me, who doesn't even like sitting on a bus seat that's still warm from someone who just got up, this violation of my personal space, compounded by what I learned only two hours ago is PTSD, has me just about ready to roll down the window and jump out. But I can't; because this woman is so close, I don't even have enough room to move my arm. Doing all I can to distract myself from the fact that I need space and I need it now, I try to focus on outside. For some minutes, I watch my breath mist

127

over the glass until it obscures the ancient citadel. When it fades away, I catch her reflection on the tinted glass trying to adjust her seat belt.

"Oof," she says, giving it a yank.

I turn my head just in time to witness her tizzy irritation, a flush in the region of her third chin. After a few more good tugs that rock the car seat and threaten to dislodge my ribs, the belt is finally swallowed up under the rolls of her waist. Not finished, she adjusts her prodigious posterior in the seat, just as a hen would when about to lay an egg. The old leather upholstery emits a little squeak.

In contrast to the woman next to me, the man in the front passenger's seat is thin and nearly all beard, with only his eyes and nose on view. His black jacket hangs loosely off his shoulders and he holds a prayer book close to his face. He rocks back and forth, his long sidelocks moving in unison with the furry yellow dice hanging from the mirror.

"Oof!" she says, yanking the belt again. "Why do these damn things always come undone, for God's sake?"

The religious man swings around.

"What are you gawking at?" she says, looking at him through seductive eyes. "You should be talking to the Master of the Universe, not looking at the ladies." The man turns back to his prayers.

The din from the traffic is already head-splitting and crescendos when a man with a scowl on his face and a string of bagels hanging over his shoulder tries to squeeze between us and the car in front. Baiting the bagel seller, the driver edges his taxi forward. The man slams his fist on the hood. Not wishing to be seen as a "sucker," because this is considered the lowest life form on the Israeli food chain, the driver strikes back. He slams down the car horn like an over-eager contestant in a game show.

The driver's eyes dart from the traffic in front to the rearview mirror, hoping to catch the eye of the woman in the back seat.

He raises a bushy eyebrow. "How's that knee of yours, Edna?"

She lifts the edge of her sunflower skirt to reveal a grubby bandage stretched around her knee.

"Honestly, Shimmy," she says, giving the dressing a little prod, "I'll be sixty in June and when you get to my age, falling over is not what it is when you're twenty. I'm telling you, floors are not built for knees my age."

128

"It's a good job it's only a sprain," he says. "You'll get through it. You're not just a pretty face."

Edna twists a lock of dyed-orange hair behind her ear, then tucks her wayward bra strap back under her sleeveless blouse.

"Don't talk to me about pain, Shimmy," she says. "I have never been in so much agony in all my life."

You have no idea, lady, I think to myself, loathing her. By the way you're carrying on, anyone would think it was you who had been stabbed.

While we continue to crawl up to the Old City, one cobblestone at a time, Edna turns to me and, immediately making me feel guilty for despising her, asks me if I am feeling alright. "You look very pale, dear," she says in a motherly voice. "You should eat more. You're far too thin and, if you don't mind my saying so, much too weak."

Clearly, the effort it took for me to get into the taxi did not go unnoticed. Giving my hand a little pat, she says she knows how I feel. Don't get her wrong. She doesn't want to pry. She has an eating disorder too. Not the kind I have. Hers is different. Tendency to overeat. Better fat than thin, is what her Michael always says. At least being overweight doesn't damage the immune system. She pats my hand again. Her therapist says eating disorders are all in the mind.

Edna thinks I need cheering up. And what could be better than a little music. At her request, the driver turns on the radio. Out comes the sound of a Middle Eastern *oud* and the quarter-tone scales of a violin. Edna bobs along while I grip my knees. Out of tune, out of time, and unaware that I am about to pass out at even the thought of her knocking a rib, at the end of every chorus she says to the driver, they-just-don't-write-songs-like-they-used-to-do-they-Shimmy, to which he replies, they-certainly-don't-Edna-they-certainly-don't.

I try to think of puppies, kittens and rainbows, but I can't. Instead, I imagine me thumping her poor little bandaged, pathetic sprained knee.

The collective cheer of the sing-along is interrupted suddenly by an announcement blaring through the speakers. It's over to Jerusalem for a press conference of the Israeli Police. The formidable and grammatically correct syntax of the Jerusalem Police Commissioner, Major-General Aharon Franco, makes his voice larger than life.

"The police have arrested Palestinians Kifah Ghanimat and Ayad Fatafta for the murder of the American tourist Kristine Luken. Kay Wilson, the Israeli tour guide who was with her, managed to stab Fatafta, which—"

"Oh, Shimmy! I rememb—"

"Shh!" I spit.

In a motherly scold, Edna says that a short temper is caused by a lack of vitamins and a weakened immune system. I squeeze my eyes tight until I see orange dots.

"—DNA extracted from his blood on her sleeve led to their arrest. Ghanimat also confessed to the murder of Neta Blatt-Sorek in February last year. The Israeli Security Agency praised Wilson's actions, courage and presence of mind, which led to the arrest of this terror cell, who have avoided capture for over a year."

Next I hear my own feeble, breathless voice. It is the interview the media conducted with me in the hospital. I sound like an old, demented woman, oblivious to her imminent decline. Wheezy albeit breezy, it is as if I don't have a care in the world. Then as abruptly as the announcement came, it ends. It's over to the weather forecast. There may be showers tonight.

Every neuron in my brain is alight. I had no idea that my stabbing him led to their arrest. As for Neta Blatt-Sorek, I remember that story being on the news. Her body was found in the grounds of Beit Jamal, a monastery near Beit Shemesh. But as far as I can recall, it was believed to be suicide. Stupefied, head buzzing, bones aching, lungs wheezing, drifting in and out, I sit there unable to take it all in, while Shimmy and Edna chat away.

—Fancy murdering an American Christian.

—Oh, come on, Edna. Terrorists don't exactly hold a machete to your throat and ask you to fill in a form to say you're Jewish. The bastards just assumed she was Jewish because her friend was. Did you see it back then on the news?

—I did indeed. I remember it well because Michael was away in London with his mother for the whole of December. What a shame. Can you believe her bad *mazal*? Diagnosed with kidney disease at just eighty-nine? How could I forget that dreadful attack? It was so frightening I had to stay at my sister's that night.

—How can that tour guide live with the guilt of it all? I wouldn't be surprised if she put a gun to her head.

—Oh, she'll probably survive. Russians are made of steel.

—Wilson's not Russian, she's British.

—Russians, British. They're all the same. No sense of Jewish values. None of them bother to take Hebrew names. Even Michael's cousin, did I tell you he moved to London, well, he's called Christopher and he's religious, for God's sake.

Edna and Shimmy ramble on about Hebrew names and Michael's family in London and that poor American tourist and that luckless tour guide who will end up putting a gun to her head and whether that pitiable woman is British or Russian.

I can't stand it.

"For fuck's sake, shut up! You're talking about *me*. I'm the one who got away."

Edna eyes me up and down, as if trying to ascertain whether I'm a good witch or a bad one (or maybe British or Russian). What I want to tell her is that I'm not a witch at all, but I am too stunned at the news to say anything else, and as the stunned tend to do, I can only stare. And it is upon the expanding puddle of perspiration in her massive bosom that I focus my gaze.

Suddenly, everything goes black.

My face is covered with sweat that isn't even mine.

With all the love in the world, Edna has me clasped in her bosom and is stroking the back of my head.

"Oh, my darling," she soothes. "Oh, my darling."

My ear lobes are stuffed into my ears. This makes her sound as if she's underwater. From deep within the dampness of her cleavage, the lullaby continues. "You're so brave. You're so brave."

While I squirm like an octopus in a test-tube doing all I can to wriggle free, from the vicinity of the front seat I can just make out a man's muffled voice. He is saying something to the effect of, may God comfort you and may you know no more sorrow.

* * *

As the taxi turns around to drive away, Edna, whose bosom perfume is still all over my face, sticks her head out of the window. She beams, wiggles her fingers, blows me a kiss and disappears out of sight.

I hobble a few feet to the Citadel steps to sit down and wait for Mira. My head is as heavy as my bones, weighed down with the news.

I look around expecting to see Jerusalem residents thrilled with the news that Kristine's murderers have been caught. Everyone listens to the news; surely they all know? But what I see is not Jerusalem of Gold, and of bronze and light, as the folk song says, but Jerusalem of Black. In place of the violin "for all your songs" are only vendors who bellow so loudly my skin tingles. Even the scent of pines supposedly carried on the twilight breeze is an ill-smelling gust coming from pieces of rotten fruit left strewn on the cobbled street. Jerusalem is an unfriendly, stinky, crowded, noisy hovel in which not one single resident is interested in the death of my friend.

A posse of pale-faced Hassidic men with out-of-control beards pass by me. They stoop as they walk, staring at their feet, their black sidelocks swinging back and forth. A few moments later comes a cluster of middle-aged priests. Full black cassocks, dark and gloomy, brush the ancient stones. Coming by next is the group of tourists with red caps, the ones who were on the slope just minutes ago. They walk to the top of the ancient stairs. The tour guide starts her spiel.

These walls date from the Ottoman period. Underneath are stones thousands of years old, from every era, because Jerusalem is where it all began. These walls hide secrets of millennia.

She shows them how to identify stones according to the period.

The largest ones are from Herod the Great. Herod never used uncut stone.

Then she tells them a small extra piece of trivia that cons tourists into thinking they have the best guide ever. Her little revelation is that Herod dyed his hair black.

The tourists say wow, amazing, fascinating, no kidding, and snap their cameras. The guide tells them they are going to buy a joint ticket that gives them access to the light show.

Envy boils. I loathe her and her group and their little red hats. Once, I too spent my time showing people around Israel, the country that I love. Once, I too had tourists who loved to learn about my land. Now this place is no more than ravenous earth that swallowed up the blood of Kristine Luken.

I want to go home. I want to wash Edna's sweat off my face. I want to lie still under the blanket and listen to nothing but the sound of my breathing and never think about guiding again.

Suddenly.

"Allahu Akbar!"

The call of the *muezzin* rises over Jerusalem's stone rooftops with a vehemence loud enough to wake the dead. It wails like a banshee through the timeworn alleys, forcing me back on my knees. A gag, throbbing hands, a flash of steel and a knife that blocks out the sun.

"Allahu Akbar!" the Muslim call to the faithful blasts again.

Venom pounds through my veins. People are trying to hold me down. I jab, strike, pound, slap and kick at legs, ankles and shins. Ignoring the freakish wheezing coming from my lungs, I pummel away at anything and everything.

"Fuck off!" I scream. "Leave me alone!"

"Allahu Akbar!"

Someone has me in a Heimlich maneuver, holding me around the waist from behind. When I bend to sink my teeth into the arm, I notice that my sweat pants are around my ankles. I don't care. I care about nothing except the harbinger of the *Shahada*.

"Come out, come out, wherever you are, and meet the young lady who fell from the star."

—Glinda, the Good Witch of the North

CHAPTER 15

I have no recollection of why every bone throbs and every muscles burns. For all I know, it could be because I dropped out of the beak of a migrating stork and landed straight on a burning barn.

I look around to try to figure out where I am. I am sitting at a desk upon which is a computer, an old rotary dial telephone, and a glass of tea with mint leaves. On the wall is a small barred window with shutters hanging on rusty hinges. Above me is a ceiling fan with an amputated blade. The walls are bare except for one framed photo of a man in uniform with a sensible face and a chest plastered with medal ribbons. Epaulettes, or "falafels," as they are known in the Israeli services, are attached to his shoulders. Across the top of the photo is printed "Jerusalem Police Commissioner, Major-General Aharon Franco."

Franco.

I still don't understand. Where have I heard that name before, and why am I in this pokey room in which the dirty white paint, as if exhausted with life, is peeling off the walls.

A policeman with a skewed nose strides in the room with his hands behind his back. Easing himself into the chair opposite me, he looks at me with steely eyes. On the breast pocket of his blue uniform is a stainless steel name badge: Officer D. Abutbul.

"My name… Officer Abutbul," he says in broken English, his chest expanding with authority. "But you … you … must to call me 'Dave.'"

Giving it all in my mother tongue, and sometimes reverting to Hebrew under his breath, he tries to explain. Dave is Dudu in English. In Hebrew, Dudu is short for David. His American friend Steve who is from Chicago (have I ever been there?) said Dudu sounds weird in English. It doesn't really cut it, so Steve and non-Israelis call him Dave. His policemen, on the other hand, only address him as Officer. It's better that way. It gets the job done. It keeps command and professional distance. But with foreigners, it's always Dave.

Dave it is.

The uniformed official squeezes the teabag against the side of his glass. The leaves burst out and swirl in between the mint leaves to their deaths at the bottom of the glass.

"Damn it," he mutters in Hebrew. "I asked for coffee."

He frowns. This opens up grooves on his forehead that say he's seen life. He pulls open his drawer and takes out a box of tissues.

"Please," he says in English. "Take."

When I lift my shoulder, the pain reverberates in my lungs. Puffed, hot and swollen, my shoulder feels like baked dough.

For long moments, he sits in silence, twiddling his thumbs.

Finally, he says, "You good?"

"Yes," I say, unsure as what to do with the tissue. "Thank you."

He leans back and rests his hands on the back of his head. His eyes have plans. Pronouncing the Promised Land in three distinct syllables while dropping his H's as if the letter is an optional extra, he says, "In Iz-ra-el, the police wants every bodies to be 'appy."

In a mixture of Hebrew and English, Dave reels off, in an egalitarian fashion, all of Israel's minorities whom the police want to be 'appy.

"Jewish, Muslimim, Druzim, Notzrim, Bahaim, Cherkesim. Everybody must to be 'appy."

He continues. "In Iz-ra-el, the stress is more big than Chicago and some people go lee-tel bit crazy." This "lee-tel bit crazy," he laments, happens only to tourists and always in Jerusalem. He holds up his hand, and leaves a small gap between his thumb and forefinger, to demonstrate the dimensions of traveler's madness in its smallest form.

For this man in uniform, the most important thing is that I don't worry. Everything, he reassures me, is under control.

But I am still at a complete blank as to how I have come to be sitting in front of a policeman, what he wants me to say, why he gave me a tissue, why he is telling me about mentally ill tourists, and why, for Heaven's sake, is he insisting on speaking English.

It's difficult to ascertain where he is going with this. I'm getting there though. He has gotten this far in his career due to merit and hard work. He thinks his role is to show me that working in such a diverse society has given him the professional tools to deal with everyone and anyone, including me. Officer D. Abutbul is here to help.

Without warning, he rises to his feet. Suddenly, he pounds his fists in the air as if clubbing an imaginary punching bag.

"You make like this!" he says, all windy. "You make like this!"

He stops to take a breath and loosens his collar. Then he hunches his shoulders, splays his legs and like a wild cat claws at thin air.

"You make like this! You make like this! You make like this!"

Then he thrusts his right leg forward and uses his foot to kick a fictitious enemy. He does this four, five, six times, before collapsing into his seat.

For lack of blinking, my eyes are stinging.

Dave offers a smile that reveals ivory teeth too big for his gums.

"Why you attack? Why you hit police?"

He is waiting for a "why," and I am waiting for a "when." When on earth did I hit people? When was I supposed to have attacked anyone, especially a policeman? He has the wrong person.

"O ... O ... Officer—"

He holds his hand out as if to stop the traffic. "Dave," he says. "You must to call me Dave."

"Dave," I say, shaking my head, "I really can't remember."

Dave puffs out his cheeks. My refusal to comply with his friendly attitude has left him dejected. He thinks I am not playing by the rules. His wager was that if he was kind and funny, I would offer the necessary information as to why I allegedly attacked people. My passivity, which he no doubt sees as stubbornness, is the loophole in this failed bargain.

He sinks his head into his hands. Up and down, round and round, he works his nicotine-stained fingers into his forehead while mumbling miserably to himself, in Hebrew, that he should have learned English.

To lift his spirits, I give him my view.

"Your English isn't bad, Dave, really it isn't. Learning a second language is never easy. All you need to do is speak a little every day."

And this view that I give him is in silky Hebrew.

His nostrils flare and his eyes bulge. The previously benevolent face of "Dave" is now the dark mien of an ogre who is ready to throw me into a dungeon and ditch the key.

Hebrew bounces off the walls.

"You're an Israeli? You should be ashamed of yourself!" He slams his hand down on the desk.

"You sat here and watched me act like a raving lunatic, pretending you're a tourist suffering from Jerusalem syndrome, just so you don't have to face the consequences! In addition to this mockery, you assaulted visitors and attacked a policeman. Do you know what a wealth of cases I still have to deal with?" His voice becomes a holler. "Do you know how much of my time you have wasted? Do you know? Do you know?"

I don't know, but I can guess. Jerusalem's nearly one million residents are all felons in Dave's understanding, and they have not been dealt with by the arm of the law, and it's all my fault.

He picks up the phone. "Send in Sharabi," he seethes and slams down the receiver.

I stare at my lap listening to his face. He inhales and exhales so strongly that it sounds like he is pumping up a tire. After a good minute of sucking air through his teeth, he pulls the keyboard towards him and starts to punch the keys. I'm sure he is typing in seventy-two-point bold font and underlining each and every letter at least ten times.

He is interrupted by the door opening. I turn my head to see a policeman with muscular thighs limp into the room. His sleeve is torn and his hair ruffled. Scratches as tidy as music lines are engraved across his cheek.

"Oh, come on, Sharabi," says Dave. "It's just a scratch." Then he rolls his eyes at me as if to say, "Oh, men."

Dave stands up and hugs his comrade as if he has come home after being missing in action. In this embrace, the men whisper to each other for long moments. Finally, Officer Dave sits down. The wounded positions himself beside his commander-in-chief and folds his arms.

Now that we all know I speak Hebrew, and that I am Israeli, and I am not suffering from a mental illness that afflicts tourists, Dave thinks it's time I tell them the real reason I attacked people on the steps of the Jerusalem Citadel. He wants to help. That's part of serving in the police. With a hand on his heart, he swears he isn't judging me. Given that he can see I am troubled and have been under the weather, he is willing to drop the charges of assault.

"However," he says. "There is the Allah thing. You should never say bad things about Allah. We have enough issues with security as it is."

Dave looks at me kindly. "We all get upset. We all get run down. But what can I do? I have to take care of the Allah business. You disturbed the peace. You could have sparked an international incident."

He pulls the keyboard toward him. "First name, please."

I say it.

He looks up. "Really?" He chuckles. "K, like in OK, but without the O?"

He circles the keyboard with his finger. "And your family name, my dear?"

When he gets to the S, his typing finger stops in midair and he looks at me as if I'm wearing a belt of TNT.

"Wilson? As in Kay Wilson? The tour guide who stabbed the terrorists?"

139

Suddenly it all floods back: the taxi, the news on the radio, the cleavage, the red-capped tourists, the wail of the *muezzin*, the pummeling, thumping, scratching, biting.

And over each memory, I hear the pleas of Kristine Luken.

Desolate and deranged, I thump my head against the desk to try to drown out her cries. Over the banging, I am aware of my voice, anguished, gasping and gurgling. I sound like someone being throttled.

"They murdered her ... they murdered her ... they murdered her ..."

Grief writhes and gnaws, trying to break free.

"They murdered her ... they murdered her ... they murdered her ..."

In unharnessed madness, I ignore the manly voices of "don't upset yourself," and bash until my brain is numb, unable to care that I am smearing snot and drool all over his desk. I thrash until Kristine's cries disappear and only then do I rest. With mouth hanging open, I stare with head on my arms into the desktop: an unformed void that hovers over the deep.

And then Dave said: "Let there be cake."

Or that's what I think must have happened, because when I lift up my head, there is a cake on the table in front of me. Not just any old confectionery, but a chocolate gateau with an oozing layer of coffee cream topped off with vanilla frosting, courtesy of Officer D. Abutbul.

There are also twenty or so boisterous policemen with bulging biceps and pistols in their holsters around me in the room.

In this fairytale, almost magical mood, these men talk excitedly about the capture of a terrorist cell. Like beefy Munchkins keen to congratulate their Dorothy on the death of the Wicked Witch, they crowd around, eager to give me high-fives.

Dave tells me to wipe my face and gives my shoulder a little shake of camaraderie. "You should thank my Officer Harel for the cake. He was happy to share his birthday treat for our little national hero."

Officer Harel has a torso so honed it forms an upside-down triangle. He stands with legs astride and fists dug into his narrow waist.

"How on earth did you stab that bastard?" he says, all smiles. "There's nothing to you." He also wants to know, how did I think on my feet? How did I play dead? How did I walk over a mile? How did I remember so many details that helped the police?

I don't know, I tell them. I just did.

Dave beams. "You, Kay, are the only Israeli in our people's history who has assaulted a Jewish police officer, lashed out at Christian tourists, screamed nasty things about Muslims, and been rewarded with a piece of cake."

The laughter that follows his comment causes his chest to swell with pride.

Officer Harel squeezes through to hand me a letter. It is from the Ministry of Defense.

It reads,

"This is to certify that Kay Wilson was injured in the Wars Against Israel."

Although I have never even shot a water pistol, it is I, no less, who has been injured in the Wars Against Israel. Dodging snipers and hurling grenades under the cover of smoky battlefields, it is none other than I who has held the enemy in the crosshairs. This is magnificent. Unlike the status of "terror victim," I have been in a war! And I have single-handedly won that war for our country. I am now a war hero. Blue and white is in the air. Blue and white is everywhere. It is in their uniforms, on their faces, even in the cake.

"Come on, Kay, tell us how you stabbed the fucker," they plead. But they don't have to beg. I revel in their attention, welcoming the upgrade from a deranged Christian tourist to a Jewish Israeli national hero. Finding perfection in every verb and gasping with every adjective, the men gaze at me as if I am the Chief of Staff.

It was not only I who single-handedly held off invading Arab armies; so too did Dave.

He was only eighteen. Yom Kippur. Shrapnel in his ankle.

He perches himself on the edge of his desk, rolls up his pants and rests a foot on his knee. Men crane their necks. He admits there is not a lot to see now, but to this day, he doesn't know how he survived.

An officer with a bald head and a beer gut who says his name is Motti laments a bitter experience on the battlefield. About the same age as Dave, Motti also fought in that terrible Yom Kippur War. In a detached voice, he recalls poking his head out of the hatch of a tank and looking down the turret.

"The sun beat down. It took me some time to adjust to the light. All around the Sinai were black piles. At first, I thought they were bags of charcoal but then I realized they were the bodies of Egyptian soldiers."

He wraps up his war story by saying that this frightening and unforgettable experience was in no way as traumatic as being stabbed by me.

I am soaring in a new social orbit.

The laughter dwindles and a sweet atmosphere settles. Officer Majdi, who has lugubrious eyes, asks me if I remember how Officer Lilach returned off duty to take me to X-rays and MRI's.

"She felt so bad for you, she just wanted to help."

Memories of a policewoman with a kind face flood back. Pushing my wheelchair, waiting outside radioactive rooms, fetching me tea, helping me up, Officer Lilach, a total stranger, had come off-duty at all hours of the day and night.

The essence of the heroic expires as quickly as it had inflated. I had forgotten it all. I am exhausted from these blackouts.

And then I remember: I forgot Mira! She'll be worried sick. She has no idea where I am.

Apparently she does.

"She was at the reception desk," says Officer Harel. "She came in a few minutes ago. She said she came to take you home. I wasn't having it. I told her, we've got this. We're taking you home in the police van."

It's time for a toast. Dave raises a cup of orange juice.

"To Kay!" he declares.

"To Kay!" they affirm.

"To life!" he says.

"L'chayim!" they proclaim.

PART III

"And right in the middle of a chop, I rusted solid. I've been that way ever since."

—Tin Man

CHAPTER 16

The day I ended up in Edna's cleavage, the day I assaulted people on Jerusalem's streets, the day I ate cake with Dave and his band of merry men, was the day I traveled back to my living quarters in a police van with seven officers, who, while waiting for the lights to turn green, "sang" at the top of their voices.

As we drove back to Gedera, with blue lights flashing and a siren wailing, an Israeli television station called. Tomorrow morning they would send a car to bring me to their studio for an interview.

I felt very important that I had been assigned a personal chauffeur. After the phone call, I allowed myself to indulge in thoughts of a black limousine turning up and a suave driver in a tuxedo getting out and opening the door for me.

It turned out to be a rusty old Renault Clio, and the driver, wider than he was tall, wore a yellow soccer shirt, to match the furry dice of my previous ride, the one of prayers and cleavage.

I did my best to lounge in the cramped space of the back seat, delicately trying to balance a modest-yet-national-hero posture. I waited for the driver to strike up a conversation and tell me how marvelous and brave I was, that if it hadn't been for me, those murderers would still be out there committing their wicked crimes. For the first fifteen minutes, though, he didn't say a word. It was only when we came to a stop light that he turned his head. My heart fluttered with anticipation.

A knowing smile came over his face and he said, "You work at the studio, don't you?" Without waiting for an answer, he asked if I could try to get him onto one of those chefs' programs in which the audience takes part. He likes cooking, especially fish. His wife lets him have a free hand in the kitchen.

At the next light, I rolled down the window and looked at people walking their dogs. To be truthful, I didn't just look out of the window, I stuck my head right out, hoping at least one dog walker would notice my Jewish, Israeli, hard-ass, war-hero face. That would show the driver, and he would rightfully feel like an idiot. I lingered, hoping the lights would take their time so someone could spot me and then come up and shake my hand. But people were too busy scouting the ground and picking up poop in plastic bags.

"I can't stand dogs," said the driver, tossing a cigarette out the window. "Look at all that litter."

At the studio, a corrugated iron shed the size of a caravan, I was given lots of coffee and everyone was kind. With only 20 minutes until the live program was to begin, the news anchor went rushing out to buy some chocolate chip cookies, just for me. I was also awarded several soft hugs and gentle pats on the back.

That morning, my face was screened on televisions all over Israel. A day later, it was shoved aside by what was to become known as the Arab Spring.

Fame and glory were short-lived.

But guilt was here to stay.

All I wanted to do was to be alone with my dog. Even moving into my new digs in Modi'in with Mick and Miriam did not bring a flicker of light to my bleak world. Mick was a British Israeli like me. His good-humored wife, home-made in Israel, as he liked to say, would laugh that she hated cooking; like me, she only knew how to cook eggs. Nothing made me laugh anymore, not Miriam's egg jokes and not even when Mick sat down to his favorite hobby: knitting. Bald, big-eared and with knuckles like clubs, he said he knew he looked like a truck driver doing girly things.

Every hour they would pop down to the basement room to "check on me," as they liked to call it. They puffed out their cheeks, as if relieved I was still alive. Why don't I come upstairs? Just for an hour, it will do me good. Could they do anything to help, they always asked.

My therapist thought a bit more routine would help.

So a new routine was established. Once a day someone made sure I did my therapy homework. Friends would sit with me and wait for me to finish writing. My concentration was so poor that to complete a couple of sentences could take me up to an hour. In the late afternoons, they would take me outside so I could look at trees. Dr. Rozenberg said I could pick any place where there was more than one tree. I chose the boulevard next to a small shopping center in Modi'in. The building had two floors and only four shops; one sold fake designer clothes, one sold frozen yogurt, the third sold knitting wool and bizarrely also scheduled driving lessons, and the fourth was a café.

The first time I went there was with Khalil. He brought his pistol. The second time was with Ari Davidovitch. The Colonel brought his M16. God knows what the customers thought as they sipped their cappuccinos and watched me. Frozen, knuckles clenched, and with armed guards, I stared at the elegant Royal Poinciana trees lining Blood of the Maccabees Avenue until I passed the previous day's quota for the number of seconds I had to look at a tree. Then I was taken back inside and lay down until the next day, thinking of suicide.

Suicide would be a pragmatic exit out of my unthinkable past, unmanageable present and intolerable future. I wasn't afraid to kill myself. However, I knew that taking my life would devastate the people who loved me. For this, I could never forgive myself and I was not sure that they would forgive me either. So, as irony would have it, it was guilt that saved my life even as it was guilt that took the life out of me.

Crying, I thought, was a sure sign of depression. I reasoned that because I had not cried, I couldn't be depressed. I was just "bummed" that I had a good few years ahead of me before I would die. Instead of taking my life, I wished it all away.

I'm forty-six now, I would tell myself. I probably have at least two decades to go before I die. That's twenty years before the sound of her cries, and her father's tears, are silenced. To pass the time, I set a target for my hopeful date of death and tallied off the hours on a calendar, calculating how much longer I had left to live.

Every day, while I was wishing my life away, friends came to read to me. My favorite was the Hebrew-English dictionary. I loved dictionaries. Not because learning new words would enable me to show off my vocabulary, but because by the time I had learned the words, I would be nearer to the date of my death.

Skinny, my friend from guide school, read to me from *Skinny's Book of Birds*. It was his own, self-published, made-on-a-computer book, and included his photos. I loved birds and Skinny loved me. He came regularly to sit on the floor at my feet with his legs crossed, snacking on nuts and *Bamba*, the Israeli peanut snack. He would read the zoological descriptions with different inflections, from the Latin name to the number of eggs laid. Anything to spend time with me, he would say with his mouth full.

My therapist also thought that meeting new people would be good for me. I agreed. So there it was. I was "open for visitors" a couple of days a week. Like a great rabbi granting an audience to those who want to meet him, so it was with me. Twice a week, I went upstairs to meet people I had never met, people who had taken the time to write to me and express their thoughts.

But what do people say when there is nothing really to say?

It was all well-meaning and I have no doubt that if things had been reversed I too would have had no idea what to say to someone in my position either. But, for the most part, it was clumsy and painful for us all.

Some cried, some tried to inspire, some empathized by speaking of their own sufferings, some looked at me as if I was an endangered species, and some talked about God.

The worst was when they called me a walking miracle. It burdened me with guilt. If there was such a manual as "An Idiot's Guide to Comforting Survivors of a Machete Attack," then I would have suggested that the people who sought explanations from the silent Heavens turn to the chapter that instructs them to tear their hair out and scream, "What the hell is life all about," rather than skipping over it and telling me I'm a walking miracle. I wish I'd had the courage and the kindness to say, "I don't want to be called a walking miracle because I watched her die to save my life." But I didn't. I just sat in silence. Only when they would get up to leave, would I say, "Oh, before you go, I just want to say that if you ever bump into Kristine Luken's parents, please don't mention that walking-miracle bit in front of them." I would say this meekly, as if it was an afterthought, as if I was giving friendly advice.

It felt spitefully good.

Forever lodged in my memory is the lady who wrote and said she played jazz on the accordion. That got my attention. I had never come across anyone who played jazz on the accordion. Not just that, she also wrote that I had been her tour guide three years earlier. Remember?

No, I didn't remember, I emailed back.

Not to worry, she replied. She was in Israel again, in the middle of another tour. Would it be alright for her to drop by, just for a short visit, nothing too strenuous, of course. She had a card to give me from her friend, Annabelle. I guided her too, apparently. She signed it, lots of love and God bless you, Patty Mae.

It seemed harmless.

Rosy-cheeked Patty Mae spoke with a deep-Dixie accent and sat herself down beside me on the blue-striped sofa that had been brought in last week to spruce up Mick and Miriam's living room. A wooden table with a wonky leg had also been purchased to furnish out the room. Patty Mae's arrival coincided with that of Rina Cohen, a tour guide I had never met who wanted to drop by.

Rina came directly from work with one of those tour guide microphones strapped over her chin and a speaker clipped on her belt. She sat on my other side. Not knowing where to look, we looked at everything but each other. Patty Mae tried to catch my eye, but missed the timing. Rina didn't look at me at all. She was too busy untangling her hair, plastered to her wet cheeks.

She couldn't help crying, she told me, while looking at her lap. It was just too sad. It all reminded her of her dead uncle. He was murdered in a terror attack too. She pushed her hair behind her ears and rubbed her nose with a tissue, one nostril at a time. Clutching her stomach, she inadvertently switched on her microphone. Thus I was treated to the most revolting of thick gurgling nasal noises, for me as high on the Richter scale of disgusting as the noise of someone slurping soup. Rina moved her puffy eyes all the way down to my feet then back up again. She did that four times. When she tried to speak, all that came out through the speaker was the Hebrew word for "how," which sounded as thick and as nasal as her snivels.

Then Rina got up and rushed over to the kitchen. Miriam was ready. She gathered her up in her arms. Hush, hush, it's OK, she soothed, and stroked the back of Rina's head.

Plenty of tissues and a healthy slice of banana cake later, all was calm.

While Rina was in Miriam's arms, Patty Mae found her voice. She took my hand and, stroking my fingers, told me a story. One day, when she was a young child of eleven years and four months, she was visiting her grandmother's farm. At three fifty-five in the afternoon – exactly – a tornado struck. It was dreadful. Her grandmother grabbed her by the arm and they rushed through the cornfields into the house. The door blew in and a tree toppled over and crashed onto the roof. Without a doubt, it was the most terrifying experience she had ever had. Because of her own trauma, Patty Mae understands me. Of course, it's nothing like I've been through. But no matter how old a person is when trauma strikes, she knows it always robs a person of their childhood. Then she stroked my orphaned shoulder and gave me a card from her absent friend Annabelle. It was a photo of a Jerusalem sunset the color of pummeled flesh. At the top, it said, "God is sometimes silent."

Patty Mae explained for a long time why God is sometimes silent.

Just like in visits with many others, I felt encouraged to death. But behind her words I sensed her fear, that it was not just what had happened to me that had ruffled her, it was the fact that the well-meaning clichés, such as, God is sometimes silent, or, everything has a reason, didn't work. Masquerading behind the caring sincerity was the realization that if such a horror could befall someone like Kristine Luken and me, then what was there to stop it from happening to her? I could almost hear her thinking, what kind of a God is that, for God's sake?

Like Patty Mae, many people shared their own knocks in life with me, urging me not to give up. We are going to beat this, Israelis would say. Think of our people. Think what we've been through, yet we're still here. This inspiration was not only uninspiring, it made me feel that if I didn't get through it (whatever "it" may be), I would not only be letting myself down, but Jewish people all over the world. But it also made me feel important, deluding me into an elitism arising from an experience of attempted murder that no one shared.

When some people hesitantly asked me exactly what had happened, I was at ease rattling it off, throwing in as much gore as I possibly could. Then I would feel resentful. It was as if they had forced me back into the forest, to places I didn't want to be. I hadn't asked to talk about it.

How dare they!

But when others did not ask me, I felt angry because I thought they didn't care.

How dare they!

Whoever they were, they couldn't win.

I was so self-centered that one day, when a friend called to say he was coming straight from his mother's *shiva* to visit me, all I could say (while the soil was still fresh over his mother's warm corpse) was, "On the way could you pick up some cigarettes?"

He did. He also brought some food.

Because that's what Jews do.

And usually they brought a lot.

Stuffed grape leaves, cheesecakes, hummus, fresh pitta bread, salads, pasta, fish, sweet pastries, and fruit. If it was a Friday, they came with a plate of gefilte fish. Walking into the room with their trays of something or other, they would start with the proverbial "So sorry for your loss," then would eventually meander into chatting about recipes, or the army, or politics, or the high price of rent. When they left, even the atheists said, "May God avenge her blood."

"May God avenge her blood" were the only words that made me feel alive.

So because they made me feel alive, and they were an entirely Jewish and logical response to evil, I made sure that I had more Jewish objects around than I had ever had before. Beyond meals on Jewish festivals and moderate holiday observance, Judaism was not something I had done. But now I acquired a couple of mezuzahs, an additional shiny menorah, and even Rashi's commentary on the Torah. And I started to say the morning and evening prayers every day and to light Sabbath candles on Friday nights.

This felt good at first. But as soon as the candles flickered out at night, I would be back at four o'clock in the afternoon, the hour Kristine was murdered. So the Sabbath would come and go, and when it did, I felt only relief that I was a day nearer to the date I was going to die.

There was only one thing I had to look forward to, and that was meeting Dina and Amos Blatt, the parents of murdered Neta Blatt-Sorek. When I stabbed the terrorist and the police were able to swab his blood on my sleeve, the DNA sample they obtained had enabled them to arrest him and get a confession that his partner, Kristine's murderer, had also murdered Neta. Dina called me after seeing me on television the evening the news broke that the terrorists had been caught. Call it a mother's hunch or whatever, she said, she knew that they were the same murderers. The capture of the terrorists allowed a ray of redemption to poke through for the Blatts. The speculation that Neta had taken her own life had cast a dark shadow of gossip over them. We arranged to meet as soon as I was feeling physically strong enough to ride in a car the sixty miles north to their home in Zichron Yaakov.

"Like it or not," she wryly concluded. "We're related by blood."

"It's funny, but I feel as if I'd known you all the time, but I couldn't have, could I?"

—**Dorothy**

CHAPTER 17

In Dina Blatt, I expect to find a frail old woman, stooped and somewhat helpless. Yet nothing about the seventy-four-year-old is weak, bent or incapable. Her short chic hairstyle, bright pink nails and off-the-shoulder blouse are, she explains, "personal revenge." She isn't going to let the terrorists take her life too. She takes my hand and leads me through the front door into the living room. Paintings of the environs around the quaint and historical town of Zichron Yaakov cover the walls. Watercolors of wheat in the Jezreel Valley, pastel sketches of pomegranate orchards, oil paintings of cotton fields, and acrylics of the famous vineyards. There is one gap. Dina moves her eyes to a framed photo on the coffee table, the size of the space on the wall.

It is of a rugged woman of natural beauty standing on the snow-covered Golan Heights. She is wrapped up in a thick coat with a scarf covering her nose. Her hair is tousled and windswept; her eyes are dark and soulful. In the corner, written in carefree handwriting, are the words, "Love you, Mom and Dad. Neta."

Amos, Dina's husband, is dozing upright on the sofa. Like Dina, he is in his seventies, with the same inky rings around his eyes that betray the sleepless nights. Wearing only shorts, his torso is trim and tanned, but his thin, pink and flaky legs show his age. His bald head droops to his chest.

Dina tells me to sit down in the kitchen while she prepares some food. She has made broccoli soup. It was Neta's favorite. Do I like broccoli? She is making cookies too.

"You look like a scarecrow," she scowls. "How much do you weigh?"

She is horrified. How can this be? How tall am I? How can it be that I am five feet four inches, and weigh eighty-one pounds? How can this be?

In the pint-sized kitchen, I perch on a stool and watch her pour cookie batter into a dish. The smell of sweet warm dough makes my stomach turn. For five and a half months, I have eaten nothing but cottage cheese and tomatoes and an occasional protein drink. To me, food smells like decay.

Eyes shining with pride, Dina says she has kept every newspaper article about me. After the capture of the terrorists, for twenty-four hours, she was glued to the news. On loops, the TV showed me, my knife, and the handcuffed murderers. The international media was harder for her to understand. It was a good job she had Nili her neighbor and life-long friend, who according to Dina had the body of a model in her youth but has let things slip over the last two decades or so. Nili was summoned to translate the foreign news reports into Hebrew on the day the news broke of Kristine's murder.

"The BBC, CNN, and even some of our own news reports said you were a tourist," she says, scrunching her face, as if being a tourist was the worst thing one could be. The rumors about Neta harmed her family. "Of course it wasn't suicide," she says. "Neta would never have done such a thing."

I tell her I was horrified at the images of their daughter being carried in a body bag through the orchards of the monastery of Beit Jamal. I remembered how the cameras zoomed in on Neta's husband, wringing his hands.

"I don't watch the news anymore," she says, bitterly. "I don't believe a word."

She wants to know why they thought I was a tourist.

I tell her that when I reached the picnic table, bloodied and bludgeoned, I cried out in English and Hebrew.

"In addition to that, the police discovered that an American tourist called Kristine Luken had arrived the previous day. It was logical that the first policeman who interviewed me – rather painfully in English – just before they took me into surgery, assumed I was a tourist too."

She says she thinks my very English name may have confused matters too, but, on the other hand, she has quite a few Israeli friends with names that do not sound Jewish.

"Upon arriving in Israel, I never bothered to change my name. I know many immigrants do, but I didn't. One day I will, I always told myself. But that day never came. I was in shock, drugged and on the edge of death, I did not have the presence of mind to realize he thought I was a tourist. Mistaking me for one was understandable."

She looks at me with deep-set eyes. None of that matters. In stabbing the terrorist, she says I have brought us a large measure of justice. I have restored dignity to Neta's name.

In the mid-May afternoon, as the faint sound of clucking chickens can be heard through the kitchen window, Dina tells me their story.

She and Amos first met in the army. It was love at first sight. Did she mention that they've been married for over fifty years? I must tell her if she repeats herself. Promise?

They started off in Kibbutz Afikim and were happy there, later moving to Rishon LeZion when Amos was offered a job.

"We liked it there too. But then, Neta—"

For several moments, she draws figures of eight in the cookie batter with the spoon. Occasionally she sighs, as if stirring up memories of her once-little girl, hovering beside her mother. She hopes I like chocolate chip cookies. They were always Neta's favorite, at any age.

After the murder of their daughter, they had to sell their house and move to Zichron Yaakov. All that mattered was for them to be near their granddaughter. Amos would have it no other way.

She opens the drawer and hands me a CD. On the cover is a young man in his late thirties, with tousled hair like Neta's, bright eyes and a boyish face. He sits on a stool playing a guitar.

"That's Noam," she says with pride. "He's our youngest. He's a musician in Australia. His music is the only thing that helps me sleep. My thoughts and fears are just too much. Did I tell you that he flew over here for Neta's birthday and—"

157

She stops in her tracks. "He went to her funeral instead."

I learn that Eran, her other son, has a small farm a few miles away and makes his own elderberry jam. Before I leave, I must remind her that it's in the fridge. It's organic. It will be good for me.

Without holding onto anything for balance, Dina climbs up on a stool to ferret about in the top cupboard. Her hand movements are energetic, her expression fierce.

"Amos has hidden my cigarettes again. I've been smoking for fifty years. I'm not about to stop now."

With mischief in her eye and cigarettes in her hand, she climbs down. She lights one. A line of smoke drifts upwards and disappears. When she speaks, her voice is deep and trembling.

"Let me tell you about that night. Neta went down to spend the weekend at Beit Jamal. She loved that little Salesian monastery. It's very popular with Israelis. The convent there is pretty too. The music concerts, the pottery, the homemade wines, the fragrant oils – she loved it all. Everything about it interested her."

She sucks hard on her cigarette. When she exhales, barely any smoke comes out.

"It was a stormy night. The rain was beating so hard, I thought it was raining sideways. The wind howled and howled. At eleven at night, the phone rang. It was Neta's husband, Amotz. Neta hadn't been in touch. He had spoken to the nuns. They went to her room and saw that her plate of food was untouched. He immediately called the police, who sent out a search party. He went to join them and look for her. He dropped off Noga with us – did I tell you they have a daughter – and drove down in the storm. We wrapped her up in a blanket and stroked her head until she fell asleep. All night we waited, listening to the rain. Finally, at dawn the phone rang. Amotz's voice was as stark as the wind."

She sighs so deeply I think that for her to inhale again will demand extraordinary willpower. Her cheeks are sunken with grief. "How on earth could we tell Noga? She was only eleven." Cigarette ash drops to the floor. She looks across at her husband. "He's awake. Go over. He needs you."

I shuffle over to sink into the sofa beside Amos Blatt. He puts his arm around my shoulder and pulls me near. Like his chest, his arm is covered with fine white hair soft as down. For several minutes we sit just breathing together, staring at the photo of his daughter – a child who will never return.

Amos removes his arm and holds my hand in both of his. Then he takes it and rests it against his face. His cheek is warm and grainy.

"Arabs came to her funeral, too," he croaks. "They wept alongside Jews." His warm tears fall on my fingers.

From the kitchen, Dina raises her voice. "Neta never cared what religion or race you were. If you were an Arab, she wouldn't even notice."

Amos hoists himself up. Shoulders stooped and arms hanging loosely, he drags his feet towards the armchair and lowers himself into it. Dina comes in to massage his shoulders. Why has he left his undershirt lying around again? He was always so neat. In all their more than fifty years of marriage, she never had to pick up a sock. Not anymore.

As if he cannot hear, she tells me he forgets things because he is too busy waiting for Neta to walk in the door. She describes his eyes that once twinkled and now are like smoked glass.

I watch them well up until heavy tears fall down his cheeks. His eyes become dry again. He closes them, and soon he is asleep, breathing heavily.

Dina tiptoes to the window to close the shutters. In place of the bleaching afternoon sunlight is a warm and lemony glow from a lamp in the corner of the room. It lights up the top of the wall and spreads onto the ceiling. For several moments, Dina stands in its shadows talking to herself. She will let Amos sleep. It's best that way. He'll wake up in the evening and watch TV all night. That way he won't disturb her with his tossing and turning in bed. We'll eat alone, she decides.

She comes to sit down in the armchair. With enviable dexterity, she lifts up her legs and tucks her feet under her thighs.

"Why didn't you bring your dog?" she says. "You know this is your home."

I am barely able to get the words out. When I do, they bounce off the walls. *She was run over,* I hear again and again, an endless echo. I look at the yellow lamp and wish I could disappear into its endless light. In a choked voice, I manage to tell Dina that a month ago, when one of the neighbor's children took her for a walk, Peanut slipped out of her leash into the tires of an oncoming car. On hearing this, Dina lights another cigarette. Smoke splutters out of her mouth with every syllable. I should get another dog. She got Amos a dog. It does him good. He called it Boogie. He has to feed it, take it out and care for it. He's so worried that something will happen to it that he yelled at her this morning when she told him Boogie must be taken to stay with their granddaughter, because I am bringing Peanut.

She takes another drag. "You feel guilty, don't you? You've cried about your dog and not your friend."

Dina is right. I barely knew Kristine. On the other hand, Peanut had been with me for six years. Whether sleeping by my side, going out for walks, or sneaking into hotel rooms under the cover of giggling tourists, my dog and I were never apart. Kristine and I had only spent a number of days traveling together in Poland. There had been phone calls leading up to her visit to Israel and then her late-night arrival, when we chatted only briefly before, exhausted, we each went to bed, followed by a few hours of touring before her abrupt death. I don't even have a photograph of her, not from Poland, nor from any of the places we visited on her last day alive.

It is a simple equation. I miss Peanut because I remember her life. I did not spend enough time in Kristine's company to remember and treasure hers. All I can recall are her final moments, with all their gore. And even then her death feels dreamy and theoretical. The car tires that accidentally squashed my little puppy are far more plausible than a man using serrated steel to chop up my friend.

Crying for Peanut is not only guilt-inducing, it is unpredictable and embarrassing, because it usually happens in a public space. It happened often when I was dealing with the endless, fruitless bureaucracy involved in trying to get my meager disability pension from the government.

The more public the space, the longer I would cry. It was an agonized howling, although actual tears never came. It would sometimes last for minutes, and always left me exhausted. One day, while sending off yet another useless application form at the post office, my eyes scrunched up and my cheeks contracted. The heaves were slow at first, then became faster and faster until I sounded like a foghorn. I couldn't stop. I couldn't care less. I rubbed my sleeves into my dry eye sockets like a distraught five-year-old and wiped my nose on my sleeve.

Crying for Kristine, that's different. I have only a dried-up well in the pit of my stomach. There are no tears, no emotion, nothing but an empty void.

Dina narrows her eyes. "Amos feels guilty because when Neta was attacked, he wasn't there. He feels that as her father he should have been there to protect her. I tell him he shouldn't feel guilty. It wasn't his fault. He has to go on with the business of living, not just for him, but for our granddaughter too. Guilt is killing him, Kay. If you're not careful, guilt will kill you too."

Guilt, I feel, has already killed me. It is omnipresent and omnipotent.

Guilt is inviting Kristine to Israel. Guilt is leading her to her death. Guilt is watching her die to save my life. Guilt is the mention of her name. Guilt is living to see another day. Guilt is Israel's chronicles, into which her name has been indelibly inscribed. Guilt is hearing her plead for her life but crying over a mongrel instead.

Added to the guilt of not being able to cry about Kristine is the fact that I couldn't go to her funeral. I wanted to go, to pay my respects, to caress her tombstone, to weep when I laid flowers on that plot of earth. Not just for her family, but also for me. If I'd been able to see her grave, then maybe I would have believed her death and even remembered her life. But if I had gone to her funeral, I would not have known whom to cry for first. Kristine? Her parents? Myself? And if I begin to weep at all, I think I would never stop.

Dina looks at me with kindness. She wants to offer me some motherly advice.

"Keep the dog 'thing' between you and me. People won't understand. It's certainly not something you'd mention to Kristine's parents."

I protest. "Just because I cannot cry about Kristine, I would never be so insensitive or dumb to mention the death of a dog to parents who have buried their daughter."

She stands up with a groan. "Can you help me set the table?"

* * *

And when she said this, for the first time since Kristine's murder, that is, for the first time in 157 days, or 3,768 hours or 226,080 minutes, I thought about something other than the murder of Kristine Luken. I thought about where the bowls were for the broccoli soup and the plates for the chocolate chip cookies. I thought about whether or not Dina uses a separate set of knives and forks for kosher meals. I thought about where the napkins were. Thinking about the mundane lasted about fifteen seconds. With my mind on other things, I was granted a glorious fifteen-second stay of execution.

It was that reprieve that, for the first time in five months, made me feel I was hungry. In that little living room, I ate my first proper meal since the breakfast I had eaten on December the 18th the previous year. The pita bread tasted as if the wheat had been winnowed, ground and baked right in front of my nose. The salad was so luscious that I knew how a malnourished rabbit would feel gorging on the greens of a meadow. The chocolate chip cookies were delicious. The soup was out of this world, even though I was never fond of broccoli.

It wasn't just the seconds of reprieve, it was the pain of the Blatt family that brought in the fresh air. Over the months, I had become consumed with myself. When I was not thinking of the torments of that day in the forest, or my immediate sufferings, I spent my days thinking of the dismal future in which I was doomed to physical and psychological affliction for the rest of my life. There was no room in my world for any more suffering – until I was confronted with the Blatts. Up until then, I had looked down arrogantly on the sufferings of others. My suffering was the peak, the Mount Everest of all terror attacks. My suffering meant you had to be dead before I felt even a little bit sorry. No one had suffered like me, I had deluded myself into thinking. The cost of such hubris was isolation and a hard-heartedness to others. With my visit to Amos and Dina, I had to acknowledge that there was more to life than me. Dina could have set the table quite easily by herself. Yet she knew that by asking me to help her, it gave me a purpose, something to do, someone to live for other than myself.

My own grief deluded me. Theirs was visceral. It was the space on the wall where the photo used to be. It was how Amos slumped in his chair and how the tears fell from his eyes. It was in the way Dina wrung her hands, stirred the cookie batter, and in those endless cigarettes. Our losses were our own to carry, but we were pulled together by the thread of our shared experience. It formed a tight-knit ball of empathy and cut loose any awkwardness.

It made me feel I wasn't alone. Someone could understand me and I could understand them. Yet it was bitter to know that our intimacy was not a natural one of growing together or sealed in family gatherings, but was formed because of blood on my sleeve, the DNA of the one who had destroyed our lives.

Dina was right. We were related by blood.

"Wouldn't you feel degraded to be in the company of a cowardly lion? I would."

—Cowardly Lion

CHAPTER 18

After my visit to the Blatts, I began to gain some pounds and the protective layer of fine hair that had spread over my emaciated face disappeared. But that cliché, "All good things must come to an end," came true a few months later when the State Prosecutor's Office called to tell me the date of the trial had been set.

September 11, 2011.

In bitter coincidence, on the ten-year anniversary of that terrible terrorist attack in which passenger planes crashed into the Twin Towers in New York City and murdered thousands of innocent people, I was to have my own Twin Tower experience. On September 11, 2011, I would have to face not only those who had murdered Kristine Luken, but also her parents.

Just as I avoided the subject when my therapist told me that, sooner or later, I would need to return to the scene of the crime as well as meet the murderers in court, I had also done all that I could to avoid thinking about the day I would meet Kristine's parents. I do not know where her father found the moral fortitude and kindness to call me in the hospital and say that they did not blame me. But I had subconsciously and successfully managed to tuck the inevitable meeting away, aware only of a vague sense that something was amiss.

The date for the trial set, the Lukens and I became recipients of communications from the State Prosecutor's Office. Each time an email popped up in my inbox, I felt as if I would pass out. Kristine's parents must have felt the same. Instead of them receiving updates from their daughter saying, "Hi Mom and Dad, all is well," they were getting the ins-and-outs of arraignments and the up-and-coming trial of those who had murdered her.

Neither I nor the Lukens used that correspondence as a springboard to explore the unwanted, inseparable relationship that had befallen us like a badly arranged marriage. We were two different generations, two different cultures, two different countries, two different religions. I did not know what to say to them; perhaps they felt the same. But now, with their arrival imminent and the court date looming, they wrote to invite me to meet them for coffee and cake the day before the trial. In a warm email in which they addressed me as "Dearest Kay," they suggested we could meet in a hotel in Jerusalem, "just so we can get to know each other a little before we meet in court."

The idea of coffee and cake with Kristine's parents at the American Colony Hotel aroused such a degree of shame and guilt that nibbling hors d'oeuvres with the terrorists in their cell was more appealing.

Up until we began to exchange emails to arrange our meeting, I had been having just one nightmare, the one in which I woke up after dreaming that Kristine's murder was just a dream. Now I have a new nightmare:

I am in a forest at dusk, looking around for a place to sleep. Strewn on the ground are broken bottles, empty tins, shreds of plastic and pieces of material soaked with blood. Around the garbage, flies dance and maggots crawl. I spot some pieces of soggy cardboard on the ground. Although they stink of urine, they are the only thing I can find to lie down on. I arrange them next to each other to form a makeshift mattress, then look for a pillow. Sixty feet away, down the slope of the hill, is what looks like a white cushion caught in the branches of a terebinth tree. When I shake the trunk to make it fall, steaming human feces land with a smack on my face.

A crow cackles, "It's your fault! You're a piece of shit!"

Then I wake up.

"No, you're not going insane," is what my therapist, Dr. Rozenberg, told me on the phone when I called her, wondering if I was losing my mind. "It is the shame and self-contempt that comes with survivor's guilt.

We talked about it, remember? Given the fact that you are about to face Kristine's parents, it is hardly surprising you are experiencing these horrible dreams."

She told me to look back on my Cognitive Therapy Treatment. Logic and thoughts over feelings, she said. She also gave me some breathing exercises and told me to take a tranquilizer if needed. So I did, the liquid kind with an alcohol content never less than 40%. The month before "Meeting the Parents," I managed, unknown to the selfless people I was staying with, to polish off six bottles of Scotch. Having recently been given the luxury of more privacy that included my own separate entrance, for the first time, my visitors were able to come and go without knowledge of my hosts. One of those guests was the delivery boy from the supermarket, who was too virginal even to question my online order of large amounts of moonshine.

Although the reckless binge pounded my liver, it accomplished the desired effect of calming my nerves. No one ever said anything about "The Drinking," though I suspect Mira had a hunch. She turned up one day with a new jazz CD and a super-size pack of chewing gum – both of which were bundled up in sparkly wrapping paper patterned with bottles of champagne. I'm sure it was her way of telling me she loved me and she knew. But I didn't ask and neither did she. She just gave me a warm hug and one of her little, omniscient smiles.

For a month, I tossed and turned, hemmed and hawed, wondering whether or not to bring Kristine's parents a present, and if so, what it would be. At first, I thought of flowers, but soon decided against them. Just like their daughter, flowers wither and die. I toyed with a gift of Israeli wine, then remembered that Kristine had bought them some when we visited the winery. Music, too, was out of the question. I could not know if what I chose would be one of the Lukens' favorites that they used to share with their daughter.

I decided on a book.

Not just any book, but one written by my knowledgeable tour guide friend, Skinny, the sequel to his *Skinny's Book of Birds*. In this new book, he had included his own photos of quirky and for the most part unknown niches of Israel, with short explanations in English. His book seemed a neutral and natural gift because I was a tour guide, so I wrapped it up in simple brown paper and hoped that it might "break the ice."

* * *

Parcel clenched between my hands, I sit on a bench between reception and the entrance of the Terrace Cafe at the American Colony Hotel, waiting for Kristine's parents. With its Western name and Eastern decor, the hotel is a popular meeting point for many tourists, and especially foreign journalists. The September sun squeezes through the white lattice panels surrounding the outdoor patio. Sunlight peppers onto the flagstone floor.

I look at my watch: 2:55 p.m. I have five minutes to practice my lines.

How was your flight.

It's lovely weather, isn't it.

May God comfort you in your loss.

I'm so very sorry.

I didn't mean to hurt her.

Please forgive me.

I don't know what to say.

I love you.

Words are all I have, yet words are not enough. Each sentence is inadequate and awkward. Maybe I should start with a handshake or a peck on the cheek. A hug is out of the question. It was their daughter who hugged them, not me. A handshake it must be. Not too firm, because that boasts of life, and not too flimsy, because that is uncaring. I will make it warm and semi-limp.

2:57 p.m.

I clutch my parcel, listening to the Greek music coming from the patio speakers. The balalaika forms the rhythmic and catchy Greek folk song "Yiayia." I analyze the chords while constantly checking my watch until the digital numbers finally change to 2:59 p.m.

One minute to go.

They said they would be punctual. I inhale deeply and stare at the tables and wicker chairs. Dotted among the tables are large Greek or Roman jars from which emerge exotic Bird-of-Paradise flowers. Like ballerinas, they stretch their necks, their tiaras reaching for the skies.

Thirty seconds before I am to meet Kristine's parents, I would like to feel as prepared as I can be. But this is not what I am feeling at all. Instead, I am suddenly feeling as if an oncoming truck has veered onto my side of the road and is speeding straight towards me. Because until this very last moment, I had not considered the implications of the title of Skinny's book.

Surprises in the Holy Land.

What the *fuck* was I thinking!

"Hello, dear Kay. I'm Larry Luken."

With my mouth open and heart pounding, and with my only thought now being, did he actually hear me say the word fuck, I observe myself, unstoppably, handing Kristine's father the parcel.

"It's a book," I say, falling off a roof – forever. I don't even hit the ground.

"That's really very kind," he says, his voice soft. "Come and meet Meg."

He leads the way as I, unable even to bend my knees, goose-step over to the table to a balalaika strumming "Yiayia."

Our table is at the east end of the terrace. It is low, made of dark oak and hemmed in by two black sofas and matching armchairs. I wait to see where the Lukens will settle, planning to sit as far away as possible. Dithering a little, they decide on one of the couches. They sit down in unison, not a hair's breadth apart from each other, and lean forward towards me. I, on the other hand, push myself back as far as I can into the opposite sofa. I wish the cushions would give way. Better still, I wish that I could be catapulted back in time.

Kristine's parents look about in their late sixties. Both are short and both have little round glasses. Larry has a thin layer of gray hair, a trimmed goatee and blue-green eyes like Kristine's. Meg has an open motherly face, bright eyes and mousy curly hair. Their faces give nothing away. They could be any pleasant couple with an ordinary life, who spend prosaic evenings sipping root beer on a porch in Texas. They are Ma and Pa. They could have been Grandma and Grandpa, had Kristine lived and had children of her own.

"It's so good to meet you, Kay," Meg says warmly.

"You too," I say evenly enough.

We smile at each other and, after a while, Larry remarks on the hot dry breeze.

"Is it typical for September?" he asks.

"Yes," I say, holding it together.

After another pause, longer than the first, Meg rummages in her purse and pulls out a parcel. Wrapped in shiny blue paper and tied with a white ribbon, it is the shape of a book. She hands me their gift and Larry passes mine to his wife, saying, look what Kay brought for us, dear. Unlike their shiny bright ribbon-tied package, mine is done up with scotch tape, which has lifted slightly.

... in the Holy Land peeks out from under the paper.

Hastily, I put their gift to me on the table, to show that I will open it later, begging God that they will get the hint and do the same.

Kristine's mother picks at the tape.

Please God, please God. Don't let her even think about opening it now.

"Shall we open it now, dear?"

Call it a reflex or whatever you will, but her question causes me to jerk forward, snatch the package out of her hands and push it across the table.

"Open it later," I say. "It's a surprise."

Surprise? For the love of God, I just said, "Surprise!" As in *Surprises in the Holy Land.*

My face has found a mind of its own. I am unable to do anything about the utterly stupid expression spreading across it. Why I react with such untamed idiocy, I do not know. But smiling I am. Not just any old smile, but one of clenched teeth, and lips so forcefully spread apart that my cheeks puff out. I am aware my mouth has taken the shape of a cartoon dog bone.

The balalaika stops. A silence of indictment blares out of the sound system as I grin like an imbecile.

To hide my shame, I swing around and pretend to be busy by searching for anyone who looks waiter-ish. I catch the eye of a young man who has an apron around his waist and menus under his arm.

Redemption is nigh.

To attract his attention, instead of a polite flick of a wrist, I opt for waving both arms with the enthusiasm of a pompom girl. Far away, I hear Larry softly telling his wife, with a little, warm chuckle, "In the Middle East, people talk with their hands."

The waiter paces towards us.

God bless that garçon's soul.

And God bless Mrs. Luken, who has finally tucked my present into her bag and out of sight.

The waiter is a clean-shaven, good-looking young man with broad, straight shoulders.

"Good afternoon, dear friends," he says in Arab-accented English. "My name is Kifah."

For a silent lifetime, I stare open-mouthed at the waiter who bears the same name as the brute who murdered Kristine.

I glance over at the Lukens. They show no sign that anything is amiss. Their eyes are attentive to what he has to say. Maybe they just don't know how "Kifah" is pronounced, because they have never actually heard it. They would only have read the name in their newspapers and the court documents. They may well think "Kifah" could be pronounced as "Kai-fa."

He hands the Lukens a menu then passes one to me. I want to take it, but my arm, in mutiny with my brain, refuses to move.

He raises an eyebrow. "Shall I put it on the table?"

Coming to, I take it from him and hold it up to my face so close that the words are nothing but a blur. I hear Larry ask if there is a particularly good cake he recommends.

The waiter rattles off the options.

"It's not an easy choice. There are so many desserts to choose from. The apple pie is delicious. It is famous throughout Jerusalem. But if I may, I would like to recommend today's special. Cheesecake with a plum jelly topping."

I lower the menu slightly and watch Meg squeeze her husband's hand. "Cheesecake sounds lovely, doesn't it, dear?"

"It does indeed. What would you like, Kay? Apple pie or cheesecake?"

I can hardly believe my luck. They haven't realized that our handsome server has the same name as a knife-wielding savage. Blood comes back to my head.

"Apple pie or cheesecake?" the waiter says.

"Yes, thank you," I hear myself say.

My remark ignites our server's professional ambitions. As if his salary is dependent upon how much I will eat, he runs through the additional delicacies.

Freshly baked brownies, coffee gateau, chocolate croissants, blueberry muffins, banana bread with almonds. The crème brûlée is exquisite too. There is also a marvelous selection of Italian sorbets that sit very nicely on the palate with Arabic coffee.

"Yummy," I say.

On rare childhood occasions, when untouched vegetables were ousted in favor of dessert, I may have used this word, but as an adult, I swear – with my hand on my heart – that I have never said it. Never. It's just not me. "Delicious," "tasty," "scrumptious" or "mouth-watering" would be my normative choice concerning matters of the palate. But never "yummy."

To make matters worse, I say "yummy" in my best jolly voice.

The waiter leaves to fetch our order. For the second time in as many minutes, I turn so they cannot see my face. Frantically, I search around to fake interest in something. Anything. Anything at all to spark a conversation.

I spot a waiter polishing a wine glass.

"I've always wanted to do that," I say.

Although the Master of the Universe alone may know why this moronic comment comes out of my mouth, I doubt that even He would lay claim to know why I also choose to conclude expressing my lifelong dream with a choke, a titter and a snort. An infestation of something or other crawls through my every artery and vein, causing not just my face to burn but my whole body too. Any curiosity from Larry and Meg as to why I have always wanted to breathe on a glass and rub it with my sleeve is interrupted by music suddenly blasting through the sound system.

This Frank Sinatra tune, which in its simplicity was always somewhat heavenly to me, is now the song of the damned. Rigid, I listen to the mocking little pizzicatos, egging Frank on to "take a swing." And take a swing he does – right below the belt.

"And then I go and spoil it all by saying something stupid like I lu-uv you."

"Stupid" is an especially painful blow.

Waiting for cheesecake, or in my case, apple pie, freshly baked brownies, coffee gateau, chocolate croissants, blueberry muffins, banana bread, creme brûlée and the marvelous selection of Italian sorbets, conversation splutters. Kristine's parents exchange a few remarks about long flights, summery weather and plums from the Golan Heights, while I "check out" by imagining that they are speaking of how glad they are that Kristine and I are friends. How thrilled they are that their daughter is here to see the land that she loves. They are as delighted as she that I invited her to Israel.

There is the welcome squeak of wheels. An Arab called Kifah whose namesake murdered their daughter comes towards us with a double-tiered stainless-steel trolley full of dessert. He pulls the trolley to a halt.

He takes a little bow at me. "Look what I have for you, Madame. All the desserts you could possibly dream of."

The cheesecake is covered with a dark red jelly that looks like blood. He asks the Lukens if it looks delicious. The plums, he reminds them, are from the Golan Heights.

"It looks super, thank you," Larry tells him. Meg nods her head enthusiastically.

The waiter turns to me. "And you Madame, what would you —"

"Cheesecake," I snap.

As the waiter gives our cutlery an extra polish, Larry tells him they are enjoying Jerusalem and Meg gives him a "what-it-is-to-be-so-young-without-a-care-in-the-world" look.

Cake forks all shiny, the garçon places the cheesecake on the table.

"Where are you from?" he asks us all.

"I'm from here," I say, in a voice as tepid as the lukewarm glass of water on the table.

He turns to the Lukens. "And you, dear friends, where are you from?"

"America," Kristine's parents say in unison.

Kifah picks up the knife. Bragging to the bereaved, it glints in the sun. Outside of time, the Arab whistles softly while he carves, slices, severs and chops. Red goo drips from the blade.

The waiter hands us our portions and takes the coffee pot. Vintage Ottoman, the *finjan* is made of brass and has a long curved spout. From a foot high, he pours thick black coffee into thimble cups. After passing me one, he offers one to Meg, pleasantly remarking to Larry that his wife has beautiful eyes.

"How many camels would you like for your dear lady?"

Kristine's father puts his arm around his wife and jokes along politely. His wife is not for sale, no matter what sheikh on a white stallion is interested or how many camels are offered.

Kifah gives a little laugh. "That is understood, good sir. I will therefore settle for any of your daughters instead, should Allah have so blessed you."

Minerva's owl takes wing. Swooping into the air, it flaps over Kristine's father, who looks down at the Jerusalem stones that had beckoned his daughter to her death. Then it glides over Kristine's mother. Minutes ago, Meg had commented how beautiful the Bird-of-Paradise flowers were. Now she stares at them with watery eyes.

Larry finally looks up. His eyes are vacant, his smile waxy.

"If we could have the check too, that would be appreciated."

Kifah takes another bow and leaves.

We all poke our cakes around our plates. The chink of cutlery is akin to the shattering of glass. Our pleasant typical-for-September breeze is not doing its job. I want it to pick up and turn into a tempest and sweep me away. Occasionally I risk a peek at them. They don't look at me. Why did Larry loosen his collar? What am I to make of Meg now smoothing out her pants? What are they thinking? Maybe they are thinking again of how they discovered their daughter's death on the Internet, or how they had to inform other family members and friends. Maybe they are remembering what it was like to sort through her belongings, to go through her personal emails – which must have felt like voyeurism – to take care of her finances, choose wood for her casket, an epitaph for her tombstone, and have their once-little girl shipped back in a box to the USA.

Without realizing it, without even tasting it, I have gulped down the cake.

Kristine's father puts down his fork and folds his hand around his wife's. When he tells me that they are so thankful to me that Kristine's last hours on this earth were happy ones, I want to curl up and die. It was I who led her to her death. Kristine is dead because of me. I watched her die to save my life. It's a simple equation. If I had not been born, she would still be alive.

Meg reaches over and takes my hand. "You must live, Kay. You must live. It is what Kristine would have wanted. It's what we want."

Larry puts his arm around his wife. In silence we sit, Meg holding my hand and Larry holding his wife. All I want to do is tell these pale and pained people that I am so, so sorry. I want to ask for their forgiveness. More than anything, I want to throw my arms around them, bawl in their necks and tell them I wish it had been me.

But I can't.

Not here.

Not in public.

Not in the Terrace Cafe.

Not in the American Colony Hotel.

Because if I do, I will wail and howl and cry and scream and never stop.

But if I don't say something, they will think I'm a psychopath. I must say something. Anything, anything at all.

So I say,

"I know how you feel."

I elaborate.

"I lost my dog. Her name was Peanut. She was a cross between a Pinscher and a Jack Russell."

PART IV

"Pooh! What a smell of sulphur!"

—Glinda, the Good Witch of the North

CHAPTER 19

There was only one glimmer of hope in the wretchedness I experienced when meeting Kristine's parents: the knowledge of the impossibility of ever feeling a greater extent of shame, guilt, self-hatred and idiocy than I already did. I did not bother going to bed that night. I showered and dressed in preparation for the morning, then just sat on the edge of the bed staring with glazed eyes at the spot where Peanut used to sleep. There was no pit deeper into which I could fall. Held together only by the frayed fiber of obligation to turn up in court, I was too strung out to feel any apprehension or nerves. The east wind whipped the shutters. They creaked and slammed all night. By the time morning came, the wind had died down, but the warm air blowing through the lobby of the Jerusalem District Court felt as cold as death.

The stairs leading up to the courtroom are the first stairs I have climbed in nine months. My legs might as well be pushing through slow-setting concrete. Even my blood feels as if it is limping through my veins, one capillary at a time. Linking arms with Dina and Amos Blatt, I am aware that Kristine's parents are behind me. I hear their hollow footsteps on the glaring white stairs, but I dare not look behind. All I can hope is that Skinny and The Colonel, who have assigned themselves to help them with anything they need, are helping them keep their minds off idiotic, psychopathic, heartless, braindead me.

At the top of the stairwell my indifference to what is to come disappears. Stomach fluttering and knees trembling, I edge nearer to the room in which I will face those who tried to murder me. After nine months of snail-paced judicial bureaucracy, the gavel will slam and they will be locked away.

We are met by a handful of security guards. One group encircles me and the Blatts, the other the Lukens. There is not even enough time to ask myself what is happening when suddenly, from the far end of the corridor, a stampede emerges. Pushing and shoving their cameras and microphones in the air, the herd of journalists and cameramen makes a beeline for us.

A microphone on a pole hangs over our heads. Are you scared to see them, Kay? Tell us how you're feeling. What about you, Dina?

"I have nothing to say to some of you," Dina says, with a good bit of chill.

There are no further questions from the "some," those who had indulged in the speculation of suicide. Not even the ones who peppered their questions with "please," or "could you," or "would you mind." None. Not one. But to the chosen few, Dina tells them she feels as if she is about to enter the eye of the storm.

A security guard with a pink face that has not yet seen a razor shoos the media away.

"You know the rules," he says. "No cameras in court."

Watching the journalists disperse, the guard tells us his name is Israel, and just like his namesake, he can do anything. Israel tells us we are to wait where we are while he goes to check what room we are in.

Thumbs in his belt, he swaggers down the corridor stopping to read the sheets of paper slid into plastic pockets on the wall beside each door, lists that bear the names of the judges, the offenders and the trial times.

"Over here," he calls out, a few doors later.

Far from the grandiose courtroom I had imagined, this one has no oak furniture, high ceiling, or a gallery. Haphazard benches fill a space with whitewashed walls that, even if everyone is crushed in, can hold no more than forty people. It looks like a bomb shelter. At the end of the room is a cheap Formica bench about five feet high that stretches the twenty or so feet from one wall to the other. On it are three old computer monitors and tangled wires. Centered above all this and pinned to the wall is a lopsided shield of a menorah, the emblem of the State of Israel.

Israel points to my place for the duration of the trial: a bench too big for one but not quite big enough to seat two comfortably, adjacent to the judges themselves.

"You will sit over there," he says, blushing with pride.

As I follow Israel across the small room, he glances behind three times to check I'm still with him. When I sit down, the mild-mannered guard squeezes himself in beside me. He chats about the people who have a variety of tasks to perform during the trial. Occasionally he raises his voice to beat the crescendo of Jerusalem traffic coming through a small barred open window.

"I'm telling you, Kay, the stenographer is a legend in her lifetime. She types faster than anyone in the country. The Arabic translator is great too. They pay shit here, though. She has to work in a kindergarten just to make ends meet. The judges are alright. No one gets excited about anything here. They're all used to this."

The bench opposite me is where the murderers will be. Between me and them, there will be no guard or enclosed glass booth or anything else obstructing my view. There will be nothing but fifteen feet of space.

Dina and Amos sit in the front row. As if I don't already know, Dina tells me the Lukens are sitting in the back with Mira. There's no official English translator, so Mira has volunteered to do the job herself.

Dina turns to Israel. "It's so stuffy in here," she says. "Amos will die. Can't you turn on the air conditioning?" She clutches her throat to show how Amos may die.

The guard bites his lip. He doesn't know that he can do that, so Dina gives him look that says, *But you're Israel, Israel can do anything.*

Israel struts off to sort it out. Never should it be said that turning on the air conditioner is the one thing Israel cannot do.

The trial is to take place in an open court, which means that any member of the public can attend. Over the hum of traffic, people breeze in like tumbleweed, carrying cups of coffee while complaining in barbed Sephardi, Russian and American accents about the price of parking or the vending machine downstairs that gobbles coins three times the worth of the drink before it decides whether or not to dish it out. Others muse about the cloudy day with its *sharav*, the heat-wave typical-for-early-September-is-it-not. Some offer me a timid smile, or a thumbs-up, and others clench their fists at me as if to say, "Be strong. We're with you."

Jews, Druze, Muslims and Christians, people from all walks of life in Israel, have come to show they care, even though most have probably never been to, nor had even heard of, Horvat Hanut until the blood of Kristine Luken put it on the map.

Like a man who knows what he wants in life, Khalil elbows his way firmly through the people milling around, those thankfully obscuring my view of Kristine's parents. In his pinstripe suit, shiny shoes and pink tie, he is the only one in formal dress. He introduces himself to Dina and Amos. He tells them he is glad to be here for them as well as for me. Why is he dressed for a wedding, Dina wants to know.

He offers her his hand. She eyes his ruby ring with suspicion.

"It's real," he says and stuffs his hands in his pocket.

Would they mind moving one space over? That way he can sit on the end and be next to me and also to her. How is she feeling, Khalil asks Dina. She is feeling sick. She wants this day to end.

Erez Padan, the State Prosecutor, has eyes as black as his robe, a bony pale face with a confident jaw and lips no wider than a line in the sand. Although we have spoken on the phone, this is the first time we are meeting in person. I long for there to be a courtroom brute underneath his prim and courteous manner. His little wooden desk with its wobbly legs is adjacent to my seat. Busying himself with his documents, he reminds me that with the confession of the terrorists, my testimony, and the forensic evidence, the trial is only a matter of procedure.

"However," he adds, not looking up, "this is Israel."

With that, the chatter suddenly stops, coinciding with a lull in the noise of traffic coming through the window. It leaves a silence so thick that I could be in a soundproof cell with lead walls.

The door opens. Heads turn. I hear the chains around their legs clink. I swing my eyes away, back to the empty chairs at the judges' bench, to the monitors, the cables, anything but to look at *them* come into the room. A creak. Fifteen feet away, I hear the demons take their seats.

"All rise," someone says, in a voice of I-suppose-we-should-seeing-as-we-are-already-here. Three judges come through a side door and ease themselves into the padded office chairs. In the middle chair, a judge with silver hair as wild as his eyes scowls across at an empty desk. He turns to the judge on his left, a man with high cheekbones and greased black wavy hair who looks faintly like Elvis. Does he know where the Defense Counsel is? Elvis shrugs. The other judge, a woman with horn-rimmed glasses and pursed glossed lips, frowns. No, she doesn't know where he is either.

Suddenly the door opens. I keep my eyes averted from the demons as a skinny man with a greased-back ponytail hurries to the empty desk. His face is unshaven. Under his open gown, which stops way short of the ankles, is a pair of jeans and sneakers. He looks more like a man who works in a second-hand car office decorated with calendars of scantily clad women than the Defense Counsel of the State of Israel. He coughs a deep, thick, smoker's cough, fumbles in his pockets and pulls out a tissue. He spits out the phlegm. Lungs all clean and sparkly, he starts to explain about the problems of parking, but his words are overridden by the chief presiding judge.

"Yes, we know that already," the judge says, his voice dragging. "Prosecution, state the case."

Over the sound of rumbling buses coming from the little barred window, Erez Padan snaps open his file. He rustles his papers, gives a little cough, then, as if reading from the Bible, says,

"There are five indictments against the accused. All indictments pertain to the accused Kifah Ghanimat, indictment number five pertains to both the accused Kifah Ghanimat and also to the accused Ayad Fatafta."

He outlines the first indictment, which tells how Kifah Ghanimat knew a woman from Beit Shemesh. She used to buy fruits at his market stand, where he sold chickens. He led her to a cave near the monastery of Beit Jamal, tied her hands and left her there alone. He returned later, put a knife to her throat and forced her to undress.

The Prosecutor concludes with the statement, "He penetrated her sexually." Not forced himself upon her, humiliated her, raped her, destroyed her life, just "penetrated her sexually."

Padan turns the page. He reads out the second indictment.

"The accused Kifah Ghanimat illegally entered Israel and made his way to Moshav Zecharia, broke into a house, and stole a safe, out of which he took a pistol, bullets and money. A few days later, he used the pistol to shoot at Jews and also at an army jeep. Nothing was hit and no one was hurt."

Without a pause, he moves on to the third indictment.

Not even a year passed, before the accused Kifah Ghanimat decided to try to "murder Jews again." He took a knife, illegally entered Israel, went to Beit Shemesh, and stabbed two young adults in the stomach.

Slimy and odious, their evil slides over me like oil. It is sickening and tangible. Losing count of their monstrous deeds, I can barely recall how many indictments we have heard. It must be three. One is the rape. Two is the shootings and three is the stabbing. It's four now. It's Neta. And then me.

One bus, two buses, three buses. Padan waits for the traffic to subside.

"On February 23, 2010, the accused Kifah Ghanimat entered Beit Shemesh planning to steal a car. He picked up the recently convicted Ibrahim Ghanimat. They broke into a house, stole car keys, phones and documents, then drove to Beit Jamal. At around 17:00, they saw Neta Blatt-Sorek. Neta was taking a walk in the area. They decided to murder her. They said it was revenge for the Palestinian situation. The two seized the frightened Neta, and then they led her to a hidden place in the forest."

Dina clutches her husband's arm. Amos' face is stone. Mouth slightly open, he stares ahead with glazed eyes.

"They stabbed Neta twice in her chest, then took a rope, wrapped it around her neck and strangled her."

It's indictment number five. It's me. Blood drains from my face. I squeeze my eyes shut. The voice of the Prosecutor rings out in court.

"On December 17, 2010, the accused Kifah Ghanimat and the accused Ayad Fatafta entered Israel in order to murder Jews, for which purpose the two brought knifes with them. The next day, near Moshav Matta, they noticed two women, Kristine Luken and Kay Wilson, and decided to murder them. The accused Kifah Ghanimat seized Kristine Luken and the accused Ayad Fatafta seized Kay Wilson. The two women pleaded for their lives but the two tied their hands behind their backs and covered their mouths. The accused Kifah Ghanimat stabbed Kristine

Luken several times until she died. The accused Ayad Fatafta stabbed Kay Wilson multiple times until she pretended to be dead and so was left severely wounded but survived."

Padan steps a few feet aside, opening up a direct line of vision between me and those who hacked at us with their knives. I hastily look down at the floor. The mottled-gray tiles swirl. The base of my skull feels like a hand is clutching it, squeezing nerve, sinew and muscle.

But not to look at them is to concede defeat.

So with my eyes I tiptoe up, starting with their feet. Scuffed shoes, soft shoes. No heels or capped toes, just kick-off-your-boots-and-watch-TV kind of shoes. Ankles next. Ankles covered with orange pants stuffed behind a chunky chain about a foot long. Bright and happy orange pants, a festive hue, not the color of those who murder and maim.

I edge my eyes up. Slightly arched, as if holding an imaginary tennis ball, a pair of hands rests on the table. The fingers tap, slowly, quickly, then slowly again. Next to these hands are the elbows of the other one. Digging into the desk, they lead up to gnarled fingers that fiddle with a watch.

I move my eyes up once more.

Those who hacked without fury, holding a machete in one hand and a Marlboro in the other, continue to violate everything that is human by yawning and rolling their eyes. There is no remorse, no regret, not even a fear of punishment. Evil fiends, they are appalled by nothing, they are already dead in their souls.

"I'll fight you with one paw tied behind my back! I'll fight you standing on one foot! I'll fight you with my eyes closed."

—Cowardly Lion

CHAPTER 20

After the indictments, I am the first to testify. When I get up to make my way the six feet to the witness stand, it causes an altercation between the terrorists. One barks at the other, who snarls back like a chained dog. They ignore the judges, the guard, and everyone else in the room who is telling them to shut up.

I ask Khalil what they are arguing about. Tight-lipped and with puffed cheeks, my bus driver looks like an oboe player about to explode.

"They're blaming each other," he says. "They've only just found out that you're alive!"

How exhilarating, bright and glorious! These are the most spectacular words I have heard in nine months. They've only just found out that I am alive! It is as if above their heads a bright rainbow appears, glowing specially for me. The only cloud of regret I have is that I did not have the foresight to write "Fuck you" in Arabic on the soles of my shoes. If I had, I would now be stretching my legs all the way across the room and wiggling my feet under their sniveling noses.

No matter how hard I try to widen my grin, my mouth will not stretch any further, even when a meaty guard grabs them by the scruffs of their necks, hoists them up, gives them a little shake and throws them back down. My head is touching the ceiling. Those bastards didn't know I was alive! I am sovereign, and they are subservient!

At the witness stand, I inhale deeply, boasting liberty and bragging the life within me. I look hard into their dead eyes. Unlike you, I am free. Free to get up, free to leave the room, free to come, free to go, free to speak, free to wipe the sweat off my brow. Never again will you make me beg for my life. Never again will you stop me from walking, running, talking, or anything else that I choose to do. I will do anything I damn well want and that includes telling every person in this room what you did to us.

I decide that if I recount the events calmly, it will be more lacerating for them. They will see that they didn't "get me." But it's a dilemma. In order for the judges to be appropriately horrified, I don't want to leave anything out. Yet knowing Kristine's parents are about to hear what they did to their daughter, how can I possibly not skip over the gore?

In the courtroom, barely anyone stirs. A few people catch my eye then look away, but most sit with frozen faces gazing at me. I feel them urging me to go on. But instead of going on, compulsive and impulsive, I glance at the Lukens. Clutching each other, they look like they are about to be shipwrecked. The chief judge asks me to go ahead. His voice sounds far away.

All I can think of is Kristine's parents. My testimony is so choked by the lump in my throat that I can barely get the words out of my mouth. Weak and shivery, my voice is frequently drowned out by the clamor of buses on the way to the market. As quickly as it had begun, my reign is over. Supposed to be a reign of triumph, it is conquered by guilt.

The judge who looks like Elvis says I am very brave. He flicks his hand and motions me to my seat. But I don't want to step down. I want to stay here. I want to do it again. I want to do it properly, to do it loudly and do it with dignity.

The female judge takes off her glasses. She gives them a polish with her gown. I can sit down now, she says, looking hard at me. So I do.

The Prosecutor approaches the bench. The pile of papers includes, as he puts it, "evidence accepted as reliable by the Defense Counsel."

"They are the confessions of the accused, Kay's interview with the police, her sweatshirt and necklace, all of which match the DNA of the accused Ayad Fatafta."

He hands them a pile of photographs. "And these are Kay's injuries."

As the judges bend forward to survey the damage, Padan goes into detail. The stenographer types as he speaks. The clicks of the typewriter compete with the traffic.

"Thirteen machete wounds, a crushed sternum, multiple fractures of ribs, bone splinters in her lungs, a broken shoulder blade and a dislocated shoulder."

When Padan is done, the judge hands the stenographer the dossier of my victimhood. She puts the photos of my slashed flesh, with the glinting staples on the welt of my sternum and wounds oozing with pus, in a neat little pile next to her purse that has sparkles on.

Next up are the victim impact statements that will be for consideration by the court in deciding an appropriate punishment. The first is that of Neta's husband, Amotz Sorek. When the court date was set, Amotz told me he had no desire to be there. It would require the unthinkable. He would have to set eyes upon those who had butchered his wife.

But although Amotz is absent, he is present in his prose, read out by the judge. The ache, his fears, the enormity of being a single parent and raising his now-twelve-year-old daughter whose mother was destroyed, cut down. The family unit has gone. His wife has gone, the mother of his child, the past, the present and the future. What happened to him he describes as a "personal destruction of the Temple."

Next are the statements of the three survivors in the other indictments; they also decided not to attend. They write about hospitalization, therapy, helplessness, fear, social anxiety, hyper-vigilance, a diminishing circle of friends, and poor health. Every statement is a mirror of my life.

Having learned that victim impact statements can be effective in ensuring maximum punishment, I invested days in preparing mine. Within the realms of decency, I felt pleased with what I wrote. It was a fair, above-average sort of prose in which I articulated my losses, something I had tackled with considerable agony over the months in therapy. In short, my statement was my trauma homework, fine-tuned and rewritten again and again. I wanted the murderers to spend the rest of their days in prison, so I prepared my impact statement as if their entire punishment depended upon what I wrote.

When the State Prosecutor asked me on the phone if I wanted to read it aloud, I declined. Less is more, I told him. My testimony would be my moment, not the statement. There was also, I felt, something gratifying and more weighty about a judge of Jerusalem's Regional Court, no less, reading out my words.

But now I am full of regrets, because barren of both intonation and emotion, the judge with wild silvery hair gallops through my irrevocable losses as if he is reading out a menu. The loss of a friend, loss of health, loss of vocation, blah blah blah, loss of a pain-free life, loss of routine, loss of my home, loss of sleep, more blah blah, loss of weight, the loss of my humanity, loss of my innocence and the loss of hope of ever being profoundly understood by another; blah blah blah.

When he comes to the sentence about my loss of anonymity, he reads the first part as it should be: "Even the intrusion from the press is something I never ..." Then, he slowly turns the page. A good few seconds pass, during which he takes off his glasses and puts them on again before finishing off the sentence with, "... asked for."

My last paragraph, in which I wrote about my endless and incalculable demise, was supposed to be the grand finale. I had imagined the courtroom would gasp, that some would wipe their eyes, and others clutch one another in horror, but all would stare hatefully at the terrorists. But the words describing my shattered life are drowned by an angry spat of car horns.

After the noise of traffic dies down, the judge thanks me with a what-a-good-effort-my-dear smile. Then he calls for Larry Luken.

In small, slow steps, Kristine's father walks to the front with a gait of not wishing to impose. He brushes by me and takes his place at the witness stand. Poised, looking at the judges, he waits for the signal to begin.

"Do you speak Hebrew?" the judge asks him – in Hebrew.

Kristine's father doesn't move.

"No, Your Honor," the Prosecutor says. "Mr. Luken does not speak Hebrew."

"Well, who is translating for him?"

"One of Kay's friends is, Your Honor."

From somewhere in the back of the room a man cries out. His voice is indignant.

"How come terrorists are provided with an Arabic translation, not to mention a free defense provided by the state, yet you can't even provide a court translator for the victim's parents?"

"It's outrageous!" someone else chimes in. "Absolutely outrageous."

It's Khalil's turn. Swinging around to face the crowd he thrusts an arm in the air and twists his wrist as if demanding a public inquiry.

"As a proud Arab citizen of the State of Israel—"

The gavel slams. Ignoring the judge, Khalil doesn't stop.

"Why has no one thought to provide an official translation? Where is the American Embassy in all of this? They are responsible. What an absolute—"

The gavel strikes again. It is Khalil's last and only warning and a disappointment to many in the room, who are on the edge of their seats waiting to hear what an absolute something or other Khalil thinks the American Embassy is.

Sulkily compliant, he sits back and folds his arms.

The female judge lowers her glasses and peers over her nose. Does anyone here have English as a mother tongue? That's what's needed. English as a mother tongue.

From somewhere in the second row, a woman with a headscarf and dangling earrings says she could give it a try. She speaks as if she is putting in a bid for a job promotion. English is not her first language, but her grandparents were American. Mom and Dad didn't speak English at home. They should have. They only regretted it later.

Not good enough. English as a mother tongue. That's what's needed.

The discussion continues in Hebrew. A man with a baseball cap tells us that he picked up English by watching American movies. Learning English this way is better than any college education, he says, although his American friends say his accent is still too Israeli.

Same response. Not good enough. English as a mother tongue. That's what's needed.

These endearing Israeli traits, in which a pecking order is absent and everyone just wants to help, have always soothed me, yet now, instead of feeling comforted, I wish people would just shut up. This is making me cringe. Mr. Luken is frozen to the spot. He doesn't even blink. God only knows what he must be thinking. Israel, the banana republic?

"I can try."

Heads turn. At the end of the third row, is a woman with sausage-shaped lips, orange curly hair, and a cleavage I almost suffocated in. Edna from the taxi ride beams at me and wiggles her fingers.

"My husband's relatives live in London," she says to the court. "Every time they come over for the holidays, I pick up a bit more English."

Edna, however, is not chosen. It is decided that a man in a leather biker's jacket with long blond hair will do the job. Sweeping his hair out of his eyes, he admits that his Hebrew is "not strong," but at least English is his mother tongue.

Bizarrely, it doesn't matter about his Hebrew. Everyone will get the gist.

Larry Luken finally begins to read, speaking about his daughter's absence, the forever empty chair and the chasm in their lives, while the guy who looks as if he just happened to swing by on his motorbike at the last moment, with nothing better to do than go see what's up with a couple of murderers, translates.

Her father says his daughter's name, that name they once whispered when they rocked her in her cradle, the name they called to tell her to come inside from playing with her friends, the name that rang out in a university auditorium, when she stood in cap and gown with parents proudly looking on. He speaks her name, the name her executioners did not even know.

His grief is grievous, devastating and endless, causing me to feel that I am the one on trial and not the two terrorists fifteen feet away. My face burns, and drops of sweat tickle my back. Frantically I look away from him and search for a place to rest my eyes. I catch sight of something so unforgettable, so heinous and so otherworldly, that the blood rushes down to my feet and I feel I may pass out.

Those who murdered Kristine Luken are smirking at her father. To them, the incalculable pain they have caused him is nothing but a childish prank. Their evil is sizzling, their contempt is caustic, and the more Mr. Luken speaks the more they grin.

I glare vengefully at their ugly, evil faces, and beg Heaven to purge every molecule of their filthy, nauseating selves from my soul.

My rage is so visceral that the only way I can stop myself from leaping across and attacking them is to imagine that I am doing just that.

In my mind, I stride towards them with footsteps so thunderous that the floor quakes. I hop up onto their bench. Legs astride, I leer down at those who executed Kristine Luken.

Get on your knees, I order. I savor the spittle seething through my teeth. My machete is a serrated cleaver, a jagged beast over two feet long. It is delicious imagining them beg for their lives and watching them piss their pants. I examine my options. I could cut off their heads in one swoop, or saw them off at their throats. Or, I could cut half through their necks and finish them off by tearing their heads off with my bare hands. Whatever I do, I will smoke while I am doing it. Like them, I will suck on a cigarette, and tell them, *me good, me not kill.*

The back of the neck it will be.

I raise the machete. Steel glints glorious white as I hold it above their heads. Finally, I go for the kill.

Swing.

Slash.

Hack.

Chop.

Thud.

Their heads hit the ground and roll to a standstill at my feet. Frozen, grotesque, their faces are nothing more than yellow teeth biting salmon tongues and lifeless eyes staring dreamily up. It's not enough. I want more. I gouge out their eyes with my bare hands.

Squelch.

This delicious scenario is interrupted briefly when Kristine's father brushes by me on his way back from the podium. Head drooping, he looks down at his feet. Seeing him like this compels me to relive the scene again.

I do so looking up at the window, watching dark clouds pass by. Each time I relive it, it is gorier than the previous time.

Hacking heads off is not enough. I need to saw across their throats as slowly as I can and with a blunt knife. It will hurt more that way. Further, squelching out eyeballs is not enough. I need to stick pins in them.

The best part of all of this is that when the bastards are dead, somehow in this magical world, they still feel the pain.

Basking in this bloodbath is not done with impunity. My trip to hell has an entrance fee. Bent double, I clutch my stomach. Mutilated by rage, I feel I am rotting to death.

A hand touches my shoulder. I look up. A stout man in a pinstripe suit tells me the court is in recess. I look hard into his eyes. I know who he is but I can't remember his name.

"Going so soon? I wouldn't hear of it. Why, my little party's just beginning."

—Wicked Witch of the West

CHAPTER 21

As we made our way down to the cafeteria of Jerusalem's Regional Court, the *sharav* that unnerved us all was breaking. The dry gusts of air, the harbinger of the end of summer, that had swept through the stairwell only hours ago, were now cool. On the steps, I bumped into Edna. She gave my cheeks a little pinch and told me I had picked up some weight. She said she was so glad to have met me in the taxi that day. She felt it was special, as if she was the first to know the news. She couldn't stop to chat. She was already late. Michael was picking her up. He didn't want to park. Anyway, she added, it's not that he could park if he tried. She could do a better job than him, and she doesn't even drive. Then she gave my cheeks another little pinch and on the back of a napkin scribbled her name and phone number and told me not to lose it. Five steps later, the leather-jacketed man who translated for Kristine's father also wanted to say goodbye. He wished me luck and asked me if I had I ever been on a Suzuki EN500. His bike is turquoise. It's the envy of his friends. If I like motorbikes he would love to take me for a spin. He gave me a peck on the cheek and said the whole of Israel was proud of me. I blushed and so did he.

In the cafeteria that stank of cheese, a sour-faced man in an apron was operating a toaster oven for the staff lunch break. Every few minutes the oven gave a shy ping. The man opened the cheese-splattered door, slapped a slice of pizza on a piece of cardboard and slid it across the counter. We

197

could have been in some cheap pizzeria, rather than twenty feet below the room in which, minutes ago, Kifah Ghanimat was found guilty of the murders of Kristine Luken and Neta Blatt-Sorek and sentenced.

The Lukens, the Blatts, the State Prosecutor, Hannah, Mira, Skinny, Ari Davidovitch and I huddled around a table covered with yesterday's coffee stains. I understood that Kifah Ghanimat had been sentenced, but I had no idea about anything else and was too embarrassed to say so. Indulging in raging fantasy, I had missed it all. I did not even hear what his sentence was, or hear the sound of the gavel, or the clinking of chains as they were both led away. Most regrettably of all, I had missed the look on their faces.

Khalil fussed. Was I alright? Did I want coffee? Coke, water, orange juice? I opted for none of them. I felt a little sick, is what I told him, trancelike. Inside, my tempest of fury had lulled somewhat. In its place was a muted me, a meek me, but it was an uneasiness in which my placid outside was at odds with my inside.

Too ashamed to admit that I missed everything because of my raging fantasies, I tried to follow the conversation, piecing it together while hoping for someone to blurt out details of the sentence, but by their behavior I began to doubt that he had been sentenced at all. Kristine's parents still spoke softly, Dina still sighed, and Amos still stared with glazed eyes. I wondered if rage had also wrung them dry. I didn't think it had, or at least if it had, they hid it better than I did.

Before the oven pinged with our pizzas, the news was in the headlines. I scrolled on Hannah's phone, dodging advertisements about travel, wine and real estate, trying to catch up. When I saw the headlines, I opened the article. I read that Kifah Ghanimat had admitted to murdering Kristine, accepted a plea bargain, and was sentenced to … Without warning, a game application opened. Round black critters with fat yellow beaks dropped huge cream eggs on little happy bluebirds, which obligingly exploded, feathers flying everywhere.

It always does that, Hannah said, grabbing the phone. She told me that Gideon had been playing with it again. When she restarted the phone, the damning verdict and the words of the judge appeared on the screen.

Kifah Ghanimat, you are convicted of a list of offenses including rape, illegal entry into Israel, breaking into houses, theft, transporting weapons, trading weapons, four attempted murders and two murders.

198

There are no words to describe your premeditated evil and cruelty. You did not come to seek work and it is doubtful if you came to seek revenge. You are evil for evil's sake, cruel and indifferent. You revealed endless wickedness, slaughtering women with a butcher's knife, ignoring their pleas. If it were not for Kay Wilson who pretended to be dead and therefore survived, you would probably still be walking free today, harming other innocent victims. In your case, there are no mitigating circumstances. The number of offenses, and their premeditated cruelty, long duration, and their terrible results, demand consecutive sentences. The victims' cries still echo, not only in the imagination, but rise through the immense pain of their families as expressed in the impact statements and the other things we have heard in court. In light of the above, we sentence the accused, Kifah Ghanimat, to two life sentences plus 60 years consecutive imprisonment.

There was no sentencing of Ayad Fatafta, because he claimed the murder was not premeditated. He said Ghanimat had influenced him. The incredulous beast was denying responsibility.

Erez Padan explained.

The necessity to prolong the hearing was the predator's way of exerting delusional power. It was better to use up Israeli public money in a trial than go quietly. He would get more adulation from other terrorists that way. The now-convicted murderer Ghanimat was to be used as a "hostile witness" for the prosecution against Fatafta. Padan also thought that, so as to waste more time and frustrate everyone, Ghanimat would probably claim he could not remember anything. Padan intended to show that not only did Fatafta share responsibility, it was he who had steered the events that day. According to Ghanimat's confession, Fatafta had not been forced by Ghanimat to do anything. He did everything of his own free will. He was equally responsible for the death of Kristine. The formalities of the afternoon were guaranteed not to bring any surprises, Padan explained. Fatafta's guilt was indubitable, but he would need to show some footage.

What footage is that, Kristine's father asked him.

The reenactment, Padan said.

To me, a reenactment is something the police do to jog the memory of someone in the public who might have seen something suspicious. It can even be a job for some hopeful actors who start off as extras in a movie. I wasn't particularly perturbed.

But then I realized that this did not make sense. There was no need for actors or a reenactment, because I had been there, and I had seen. They had already been caught.

"What do you mean by a reenactment?" I asked.

Erez Padan spoke to his shoes. The reenactment was a police record. It was documentation, a film made when the police took the murderers back to the forest, one at a time, so they could show them what they did. No actors. Just real live murderers.

We don't need to see all of it, he said. Just the parts that prove that Fatafta acted without coercion.

Exactly which parts are those, I asked him. Which parts will we see?

How he tried to murder you, he said. That's the part. That's the part we need to watch. He sounded far away because of the sweat that was pouring down the side of my head and into my ears.

"You're talking to a man who has laughed in the face of death, sneered at doom and chuckled at catastrophe. I was petrified."

—The Great Oz

CHAPTER 22

A lopsided screen stands rigged up against the wall, ready to absorb the images from a projector connected to the Prosecutor's laptop. Now closed to the public because of the screening of the police reenactment (considered top security), the room contains only myself, the Blatts, the Lukens and the officials. Mira, still on hand to translate, is allowed in, as long as she promises, with a sort of Scout's Honor, not to talk about what she sees. Standing where Kristine's father testified is the new witness: his daughter's murderer. No longer indifferent, Kifah Ghanimat brims with gall. He leans on the podium with his elbows, and hunches his shoulders like a stalking wolf. His partner, Fatafta, has a new guard, a man with an untamed beard. The terrorist slumps back in his chair with folded arms, licking the corner of his mouth like a child in anticipation of the next prank.

On the ice-blue screen appears a thick white font, the quaking type of old, silent movies.

Matta Terror Attack. 12/21/2010.

Padan clicks the mouse. An image of a written document appears on the big screen. It is from Ghanimat's police interrogation. According to the date on the document, it took place three days after the murder. Highlighted with a yellow marker are the words,

Ayad told me, you have your knife and I have mine. Any Jew we meet today, we will murder.

Initial reports in the media had claimed that Kristine's murder was an act of revenge for Israel's assassination in Dubai of Mahmoud al-Mabhouh, a senior Hamas commander. But in these two meager sentences, there is not a word of revenge or any mention of someone called al-Mabhouh.

There is one *casus belli* and one only: their war against the Jews.

When Padan points out that Kristine Luken was a Christian, a tourist, and neither Israeli nor Jewish, Fatafta shrugs his shoulders. Why should he care? To him she was worthless, nothing but mistaken political fodder.

I look at the screen and read it again.

Any Jew we meet today, we will murder.

Today.

What the hell do they mean by "today"? Today, as opposed to Friday, when they were probably watching a soccer game, or today, instead of Sunday, when they would go to the market to steal cell phones and cigarettes? Today was the day when they woke up, slid out of bed, and decided to murder Jews. With a hocus pocus, a wave of a wand, and a lo and behold, the time for death had come.

Did they even know the previous night what they would do the following day? Had they planned it, or dwelled on it, or savored the idea for months? Maybe it was exciting, or tantalizing, or a temptation or even a turn-on. How did they choose the knives? Did they say to themselves, this one is good for fruit, this one is better for flesh?

Fatafta looks across at the screen with hooded eyes. Ghanimat swivels his finger in his ear, pulls it out and examines it. There is no shred of angst, not even at being sentenced. Nothing about them says they shouldn't have done what they did. Their boredom is obscene. They couldn't give a damn.

Erez Padan outlines their actions as they set out "to murder Jews." On the Friday night, they stuffed a few things in their bags. Coffee, hats, three avocados and a couple of knives. Fatafta dressed up in a stolen Israeli policeman's jacket and stolen Israeli army pants. Then they set off with their picnic, dodging checkpoints to cross into Israel and head to the

National Trail. They knew there would be Jews hiking there on Sabbath, so they spent the night under the trees. When the sun rose, they whiled away the hours and lay in wait for their prey.

Whiled away the hours means that they probably joked about how cool they would look, roaring playfully, "You're dead, you're dead." No doubt, they rolled around on the ground, laughing. At noon, they made more coffee in the forest and ate their lunch. At the very time that Kristine and I were raising our glasses to life, they were under the olive trees toasting death.

Eyes flinty, the Prosecutor glares at the witness. He speaks through closed teeth. "But in your confession you say, and I quote, 'Ayad told me he wanted to kill Jews.'"

In scathing hubris, Ghanimat picks at his cuticles.

Padan whips back through each slide in which Fatafta is implicated in the interrogation by his partner. Is this true, Padan asks him, with each image on the screen. Is this true? And each time the witness shrugs his shoulders, earning a grin from his partner.

"What a waste of time," says the chief judge. "Take him away."

Kristine's murderer winks at Fatafta and is led out of the room.

The judges confer in a huddle, then announce that there will be a five-minute recess. There is no need for anyone else to leave the room, they say. With that, they exit through the side door behind their bench.

Incongruently, this leaves us in a situation in which predator and prey, the murderer and the maimed, sit together as if we are at the movies, passing popcorn around and waiting for the action to begin.

With the judges absent, the Prosecutor examines the files on his computer for the screening of the reenactment. The image of the ancient walls of Horvat Hanut come into focus on his laptop. The olive trees are almost blue and the sky is a mustard yellow. When he clicks the mouse, the film fast-forwards. Fatafta appears on the computer screen handcuffed to an officer from the Military Police. Behind the two of them, is a plainclothed man with an M16 rifle strapped over his shoulder. Most unforgettable, extraordinary and gratifying of all is that Fatafta on the screen does not reflect the swine opposite me now, who puts his arms behind his head and rests back, smirking. On screen, Fatafta is on crutches.

It is a sight to behold. "How did he break his leg?" I ask Padan, hoping with all that is in me that the Shin Bet kicked the shit out of him.

A wry smile curls his mouth. "Oh that," he says. "Didn't I tell you?"

He takes a seat beside me. "After their little murder frenzy, they sat on a rock just a few feet away to have a cigarette. While they were smoking, you managed to get up. They didn't know you were still alive and you didn't know they were there. When you reached help, the army sent a helicopter. When these thugs saw the chopper, they panicked." He nods in Fatafta's direction. "He got up, fell over and broke his leg. He had to spend the night in the forest. At first light he crawled back home and left a trail of blood in the rosemary bushes.

The rosemary bushes. How divine. How poetic!

I want to squeeze Erez Padan's cheeks, pucker his ungenerous lips until they are swollen and sumptuous, then suck out their goodness with a fat juicy kiss. Barely clinging onto court protocol, I refrain from kissing the State Prosecutor and blow a kiss to Fatafta instead.

Not just any old kiss.

It is a seductive, slow, slutty, lingering, Marilyn Monroe sort of kiss, where my fingers brush my lips and with a slow-motion move of my hand, I launch it off towards him. It flutters across the room like a butterfly on a spring day aiming for its favorite pink petal.

In these intoxicating moments, I never dreamed that things would get better. But they do. Fatafta is enraged. He leaps to his feet and curses me in Arabic. Behind him, the bearded guard, who has muscles like pumped up balloons, seizes Fatafta by the shoulders, pushes him forward and hurls him across the desk. With an aargh and a thud, the terrorist lands on the floor. The guard hops over the table, kicks him a couple of times in the stomach, once in the groin, grabs him by the scruff of the neck, hoists him to his feet, slides him back across the table – just as a bartender does with a beer – and molds him back into a seated position.

Ta-da!

What finesse! No fuss, not even a tizzy. Like taking down a book from a shelf, giving it a little dusting and then putting it back. Watching Fatafta's chest heave, a beautiful serenity comes over me, the same sort of contentment I experience after I finish dusting my entire library.

Fatafta looks at me as if I am his whore. It is as if his eyes are saying, I have one up on you because I have seen you piss your pants and beg for your life. Fury seeps through my pores. I stare back, wishing that the hate in my eyes could strike him dead. I have seen you naked, my eyes say. That's worse than a piss in the pants. In you, I have seen the worst humanity can offer. You are lower than life, the scum of the earth.

Unmoved, he rubs his chin with the back of his hand.

I am both enraged and defiled. Not only did he make me beg for my life and piss my pants, he forced me to see something I never should have seen. He made me watch a woman being murdered while she begged to her God. And instead of finishing me off, he let me live while I watched her die. I cannot hate him enough.

The judges come back. They must have guessed something is up because for long moments they look around. Erez Padan jumps in with an I-am-ready-to-begin, but is sidelined by the Defense Counsel, who runs his fingers through his greasy scalp. He tells the judges that his client has been subjected to ridicule by the witness, Kay Wilson.

The Defense Counsel glares at me but talks to the judges. "This is a court of law," he says. "I would like to remind the witness, that we must keep matters dignified."

"Dignified?" I say, glaring back. "Butchering innocent women with machetes is dignified?"

Tattling on me is not enough; he is now offended that I upset his client. At this moment, I loathe him so much that if I had the opportunity I would throttle him before I'd throttle the murderer.

The judges are unimpressed with his moaning and so I love them. I love them so much, almost as much as my darling guard who is looking at me with a twinkle in his eye.

According to the digital date flickering at the bottom of the screen, the reenactment was filmed three days after the murder. The police and Shin Bet had worked with speed. In that time they put all the intelligence together, compared it with my interview, located the terrorists, arrested them, interrogated them, got a confession, then took them back to the forest.

Erez Padan tells the court that the conversations between the accused and the police are in Arabic. He will translate to Hebrew when it becomes pertinent. He fast-forwards the clip, making the limping, shackled Fatafta and his police escorts run through the forest at breakneck speed. They go so fast, I can't even see their legs move.

After about ten seconds, in which they have "walked" a mile, the camera wanders upwards to the cypress and pines. Then the screen goes black before opening up again on holly oaks and rosemary bushes.

It is a chilling and familiar space.

Within less than a week, the violent butcher, once intoxicated by omnipotence, is now on screen, meek and flaccid. His eyes dart and he mumbles into the microphone.

Padan translates. "I seized the one with the glasses from behind. She stabbed me with a small knife, so I knocked her to the ground."

On film, Fatafta points for the policemen vaguely to the region of his crotch, as if hoping for a little kiss for being a brave boy. On the bench, he picks at his nails, indifferent. Back on screen, an officer pokes a cigarette into the prisoner's mouth. When he sucks on it, gray-blue smoke funnels up towards the trees. He is allowed another puff, before the officer tosses it to the ground and stomps it out.

Again the clip moves with speed. Less than two seconds this time. We are now at the brow of the hill. Through the sparse trees looms the Zanoah Brook.

The microphone edges closer. "We asked the one with glasses to take off her shoes," translates Padan. "I helped her. Kifah went off to check if anyone was nearby. After about 10 minutes, he called me on the phone. He asked me to silence the women, because there were people around. I asked the women to keep quiet as they were talking between themselves. Kifah came back. I stabbed the woman with glasses, some stabs in the side, and a few stabs in the back."

Fatafta has to show them what he did. The officer hands him a toy knife with a red handle and a plastic blade. It is rounded at the edge. Pretending to be me, the policeman kneels on the ground and puts his hands behind his back.

But the person I see kneeling on the ground is not a burly man; it is me, the child at an English school, me, the youth plowing Israel's plains, me, the piano player in Tel Aviv, me the artist, me the friend, me, the tour guide. Me. It is me who is waiting to be executed.

There is no thrust of an arm, no glint of a knife, no crunching of bones, no ripping of flesh, no searing horror, no whimpering, no begging for life. The murderer taps the officer on the back with the rubber toy.

The camera zooms in on a thorny bush. My backpack. My keys. My ID card. The film runs again. Another bush. Camera zooms. Metal glints through dusty leaves. It runs forward again and focuses in on a large rock being used as a table. On it are two knives, the weapons that carved up life. Both are a foot long. One is curved and thin, the other jagged. Halfway along this serrated blade, the edge becomes smooth and tapers off to the tip.

On screen, Fatafta nods weakly. Handcuffed, he points with his wrists to the knife with the jagged blade. He nods again, yes it was that one, that was his knife. Meek and subservient on screen, across the room from me he seems only peeved that he chose the wrong blade. The serrated edge made it tricky to pull out of me without blood spurting over his clothes.

Unable to bear witness any longer, I look up. Through the window are clouds, so swollen they look sore, obscuring the sun that minutes ago had streaked across the courtroom floor. Drops of rain trickle on mottled glass, dragging the summer dust with them. Outside, the cloudburst begins, but inside it is already over. I am drenched with his evil.

The Prosecutor concludes by describing the interrogation and the reenactment as conclusive and damning evidence as to Fatafta's culpability in the murder of Kristine Luken. Even the Defense Counsel admits that he cannot contest this. He pokes his Kleenex-covered finger up his right nostril and gives it a little swivel. With his finger still up there, he admits,

"Ayad has committed serious crimes."

Ayad.

Not Fatafta, or Ayad Fatafta, or The Accused, or My Client. Informal and chummy, it might as well be Bob. He reads from a document saying Ayad grew up poor. He was frustrated. Given the "circumstances," murder was understandable, is what he is insinuating. In doing so, he is holding me hostage to misplaced compassion and, what is worse, he is doing it while picking his nose.

The plea for leniency is dismissed. The accused is told to stand. Indifferent even to his own fate, Fatafta stays seated and picks at his fingernails until the guard with the muscles forces him up.

There is a dull thud of the gavel, a no-fuss-who's-next thud. Fatafta holds out his wrists for the guard to snap on the handcuffs. He leads him away to start his fifty-five years: a life sentence for the murder of Kristine Luken and twenty years for trying to murder me.

The clunk of chains fades. The judges gather their files and switch off their computers. A woman with a bucket and mop comes into the room. She dips a rag in the water, squeezes it out and attaches it to the mop. Back and forth she sloshes it over the tiles. It is as if she is trying to sponge up the filth of those who gloated, snickered, mocked and yawned. She squeezes out the rag, like she is them and the rag is me.

I hold my head in my hands. On the floor are the shadows of those who have gathered around waiting to speak to me. I am pulled to my feet and embraced by Kristine's parents, two ordinary people with extraordinary courage.

Blood pounds in my ears, making everything muffled. I think they are saying something about the best revenge for terror is for me to live my life to the full. It is what Kristine would have wanted. I want to ask them if that is what they said. I want to tell them I didn't quite hear. But I am too drained to utter a word.

PART V

"The Wizard? The Wizard? Yes, of course. But first I'll take you to a little place where you can tidy up a bit."

—Cabby

CHAPTER 23

Unlike me, the Lukens were not interested in dishing out violence in return, or at least if they were, they never said so. When we parted that day, Kristine's parents said their only hope was that the terrorists would never be let out in a prisoner exchange. I, on the other hand, found much gratification in indulging in the delicious thought that every single day for the rest of those terrorists' lives, some greasy fat prison guard would hopefully beat the shit out of them.

But hopes were put on hold.

Only one month after the trial, the news was buzzing over the potential release of the kidnapped Israeli soldier, Corporal Gilad Schalit. Since his abduction by Hamas five years earlier, Israel had frequently been confronted with photos of his parents' pained faces, a mother and father who had set up a protest tent outside the government offices.

For five years, Jews around the world had prayed for his release. There was even a Gilad Schalit Worldwide *Tehillim* Project, encouraging people to recite Psalms daily on his behalf. In one of the rare campaigns in which Right and Left united, Zionist and human rights organizations worldwide also called for his release.

Who could fail to feel a lump in the throat when looking at posters of "everyone's son" and "everyone's brother," caged in a damp dark room, held captive by sadists in Gaza?

The soldier was a kid whose face was so tender I doubt he had even started shaving, and his parents were trapped in a hell that had no exit.

It was, therefore, understandable that I, like the majority of Israelis, had also stuck "Free Schalit" stickers on my car. Even Peanut had worn a yellow band around her collar, a symbol of the campaign. Calling for information on Schalit's whereabouts and demanding his release were inconsequential for me. They bore no personal cost.

Things were different now. Everything had become personal. There were talks of a prisoner exchange to have him released, described by some as "the need to pay the necessary heavy price." I seesawed between being thrilled for the Schalits and moved to tears at the idea of his release, to begrudging them the end to their agony, because it could be at my expense.

Kristine and I could have been kidnapped. If we had been, I am certain that thousands of Israelis would have demonstrated for our release. Nothing would have been a greater betrayal, or more terrifying to me, than to think that there would have been no such demonstration. Many of my countrymen would have been willing to pay the "necessary heavy price" for us, and knowing Israel, I would have expected nothing less.

But there was no "necessary heavy price" for us, because we were not kidnapped.

The necessary price was none other than the release of 1,027 Palestinian terrorists, many with blood on their hands, serving multiple life sentences. As far as I understood, this could include those who had murdered Kristine Luken.

One thousand and twenty-seven terrorists in exchange for one soldier was not, to my mind, an eye for an eye or a tooth for a tooth, but gnashing yellow teeth savaging, chewing and spitting out innocent lives. For all I knew, those two, who had mocked and yawned and smirked and laughed at the incalculable pain that they had caused the Lukens, the Blatts and me, could be part of the deal. If they were released, going by their sickening behavior in court, the first thing they would do before frying an egg in the morning would be to take a knife from the kitchen drawer and murder a couple of Jews.

Corporal Gilad Schalit and the relentless campaign of his suffering parents turned into my nightmare. I sweated through the days, waiting for a phone call from some government official to say they were very sorry, but the release of my would-be murderers are part of the "necessary heavy price."

* * *

For those few weeks after the trial and the Schalit deal, I spent most of the time in bed, with the sheet pulled over my head. It was not just the memories of who they were in the forest that brought on the sleepless nights, it was that moment in court when I had blown Fatafta a kiss. He had snapped, just as he had when he saw I had tried to wiggle out of my shoelaces that day in the forest. True savage that he was, the placid, cocky and bored facade could no longer be contained. He sprang to his feet and with eyes wild and mouth frothing, he cursed me. Reliving this scene of his unconfined rage left me in a clammy sweat. What if, upon release, he made an effort to find me? He was sick enough to do so and to slaughter anyone else I happened to be with.

For the first time in my twenty-five years in Israel, I concocted a tentative plan to leave the country, should they be part of the exchange deal. It wasn't just the fear; it was the injustice. If they were ever released, I would feel my country had crapped all over me. I would have nothing to give anymore or any desire to submit to a government that could do such a thing. Even if I returned to England and had to spend my life sitting around drinking endless cups of tea and chatting about the weather, I reasoned it would be better for me to start again there, rather than coming to hate Israel, my home, which I had loved at first sight. It would be a bitter divorce and it was not primarily hatred that would see to it that I packed my suitcase. Rather, it would be living with the agony of unrequited love; that, I just could not do.

I have no idea where those who had lost their loved ones to the released terrorists got the fortitude to stay in Israel. I cannot even begin to imagine the pain of Schalit's parents had he not been released, or the pain of the parents whose sons and daughters were murdered by those who were released. They are all better people than me, that's for sure.

Just as Kristine's parents had discovered the horrors of their daughter's death on the Internet, I discovered that Fatafta and Ghanimat were not part of the deal by surfing the news. I scrolled through the lists of the prisoners' names, not once or twice but several times, then called friends and asked them to double-check. Arabic names written in Hebrew might be spelled differently than I'd expect. I didn't want to be deluded into relief, only to find out later that I had missed their names due to some stupid spelling variation. I did not particularly care that I had not received updates from "some government official." The consolation of knowing that the prisoners were not lurking around my street waiting to finish me off was greater than the frustration caused by the infamous Israeli lack of efficiency found in many things to do with bureaucracy.

With them locked behind bars (at least until the next prisoner exchange), I had two things left to do: one was out of desire, the other out of need. I wanted to meet the families at the picnic table who had saved my life, and, according to my therapist, I needed to return to the site of the murder.

Even before the trial, I had wanted to meet those who set off for a barbecue on a bright December day and ended up tending to a dying person. Not only did I want to thank them for saving my life, I needed them to fill in some details. I wanted to hear how they had seen things on that dreadful day. But because there had been the possibility of their appearing as witnesses in the trial, I was not allowed to meet or contact them before it was all over.

It was in Tel Aviv, a month after the trial, that we met in a little pizzeria with soft lights and checkered curtains. For the first long minutes, we sat around our table on high stools, sipping glasses of water without saying a word. I stared into my water, swishing it and watching the orange lights move and reflect in the glass. At first, I could only risk a peek at the soft faces and watery eyes of Dafna, Itai, Guy and Sharon.

Even though we were around the same age, I felt like a baby who, without nurturing parents, would have died. Over untouched pizza with a crust visibly drying before us, we began to speak, and did not stop for three hours. Only when the waiter came over to say "last orders" and handed us a menu with an apologetic look for what he thought had been unsatisfactory food, did we remember to eat.

They gave me a photo. It was taken about thirty seconds before they saw me come up toward them bound, bleeding and gagged. Unlike the hues of summer and the washed-out tones of the middle of the day under the Israeli sun, the colors were stark, those of late afternoon. The trees were draped in shadow and stood out like paper cutouts. An orange light cut between their branches, streaking onto the path. It continued on to the picnic table before finally splashing onto the bottles of soda, cartons of salad and paper cups. To the side of the table, four children hovered around Itai, a handsome man with short gray hair, kind eyes and a square jaw. He squatted on his heels stoking marshmallows on a fire made with a handful of twigs. Like time itself, the rising gray smoke had stopped in its tracks, clouding his face and obscuring the silvery flecks of his hair. In the bottom left corner, in yellow digits, was "16:52 18:12:2010." This marked the moment that the photo was taken, the moment that the camera captured my life, as I had known it, coming to an end. 16:52 18:12:2010 divided two universes, the one inhabited by who I once was, and the one inhabited by what I had become. It was a mind-boggling image of time standing still, and out of sight and only a mile away from this serene family picnic, in a parallel universe, Kristine lay dead.

Deaf to the hum of restaurant chatter and blind to those watching me, I hunkered over the photo with hungry eyes. It was as if I was holding an ancient parchment, never before discovered. I searched for the missing link, the proof needed to emotionally validate that what had happened really did take place. I craved for the camera to have inadvertently caught me emerging from the trees. For over a minute, I stared, but saw nothing but a couple of families, food on a table and a barbecue.

Dafna and Sharon were both petite. They both had the same haircut that curved around the contours of their faces. Dafna was the one sitting at the table that afternoon. It was she who raised her hand to shield her eyes from the sun. She said that when she first saw me, she thought I seemed a little strange, but I was just someone taking a stroll with a dog.

You were just a silhouette, she said, her voice scarcely audible. Itai put his arm around his wife. With the sun in her eyes, he said, Dafna couldn't see a thing.

I learned that it was Dafna who had called the emergency services, while, Itai, a paramedic in the army, administered first aid. Sharon got the children into the cars and Guy, her husband, ventured out into the forest. Guy peered at me over half-rimmed glasses that partially reflected the pizza. None of us was armed, he said. We had no idea how many terrorists there were or where they were. It was terrifying.

217

Giving me first aid, calling the police, getting the children to safety and scouting the area in the knowledge that there was an unknown number of terrorists loose in the forest were actions that not only saved my life, but risked their own lives and those of their children. Looking after the seven kids was not easy, Sharon said, exhaling for a very long time. We didn't want the children to see the blood.

By the biting of lips, I knew that they had not been successful. Itai told me that their youngest daughter, just six years old, had managed to avoid seeing me. Unfortunately, though, after the ambulance had taken me away and he got into the car, the little girl saw her father covered in my blood.

Itai's voice was almost inaudible over the hum of chatter coming from other diners. We just told her that you had fallen over and hurt yourself, he said, his words fading as his wife squeezed his hand. Babbling, I thanked them all profusely and said that they were my heroes. Itai gave me a gentle pat on the shoulder. They weren't heroes, he said. It was just the natural and right thing to do.

They all followed the trial. The older children, who knew what had happened, were very interested in the outcome. Itai said the idea that "bad men" got locked up out of harm's way was essential for them to work through their fears. But I could see on all their faces and hear in their voices that although no one else felt the knife physically in their flesh, it was clear: The angels who did not fear to tread were also victims of terror in the forest on that serene winter's day.

When it came time to leave, I hugged each one. Not just a regular hug, but one where I turned my head and listened to their hearts beating. It was like being back in the womb. Noble people that they are, they never said it made them uncomfortable, nor did they try to squirm away. When I eventually let them go, I felt like a newborn baby. I was unable to scream, yet I was terrified of the world; it is massive, violent and hostile. And when they drove away, for many days to come, I felt like an abandoned orphan.

In a phone call later, Dr. Rozenberg said she was not surprised. There was no need to feel embarrassed, she told me. And then she told me in that special voice that she used when something hard was coming, it was time to revisit the forest. Not that it would be like waving a magic wand and it would make things all better, or anything like that, she said, but it wasn't good to have this hanging over me. The sooner I dealt with these fears, the better it would be.

The best I could do was to set the date as far into the future as I could, in the hope that my therapist would forget she had ever mentioned it. I told her I was thinking of doing it within the next couple of years. I don't know if she plotted and schemed, but later that day I received a call from Ruti Yechezkeli, the Academic Coordinator of Israeli Tour Guides. I told her my hope was to guide again within the next five years.

Five years? Ruti was not having it. In a few months, on April 18, 2012, there was going to be a Passover event at Horvat Hanut. The Jewish National Fund, the National Parks and the Society for the Protection of Nature had arranged a day of family hikes all over the country. The one in Horvat Hanut was arranged in coordination with Gidi Bashan, the ranger who came to the hospital to get information to locate Kristine's body. Ruti thought it would "be nice" for me to meet him again. I could also tell the hikers a little bit about the history of Horvat Hanut before the families embarked on their stroll down the Caesar's Path – the last path that Kristine ever walked.

It would spur me back to work, Ruti thought. Even if it didn't, my part was crucial. Only I could show people that there was nothing to be afraid of. Horvat Hanut was one of the most beautiful, interesting and unknown sites in Israel, she said. That's why I went there, isn't it? It's such a shame. Think of how much enjoyment I could give to people when they see that there are so many other beautiful places to while away lazy afternoons. Think how inspiring it would be for them to see this tour guide working in the very place where terrorists had tried to take her life.

Ruti told me to work hard at my therapy for a few more months. You passed the tour guide test, so this will be easy, she said.

Through clenched teeth, I agreed.

During the months of trauma therapy, I often wondered how Dr. Rozenberg, a young religious woman, could understand what I'd been through. What could anybody understand? One of my deepest inner scars was not an absence of empathy, compassion or kindness from others, but of being understood, of having a shared experience. The machete attack was out of everyone's orbit, even other survivors of terrorism. Not that my experience was worse, it was just different. Unlike in a shooting attack, with a knife there is no distance between the predator and the prey. Knife on flesh is more personal than a bullet. Then, there was the helplessness of the half an hour in which they held us at knifepoint, our fate swinging in the balance. Shaming were the moments of the delusion of reprieve, where I believed them when they said, "We good, we not kill." And then I faced them in court, those who hacked my friend to death. Overriding everything was the pervading guilt: that to save my life, I watched her die. Trauma therapy was not going to salve my psychological wounds, let alone heal them.

Yet despite deep reservations as to the effectiveness of therapy, over the months, I had progressed from staring for a few seconds at a couple of trees in a safe neighborhood – accompanied by Ari with his M16, or Khalil with his pistol – to standing in a copse of pines for as long as I wanted with unarmed friends. My pulse stayed normal, my pores exuded no sweat. I was able to look at any tree, anywhere, for as long as I wanted; except in the Matta Forest.

Writing about the attack was more draining than staring at trees. Each paragraph could take an hour. Should I write "stabbed" or "bludgeoned"? Did Kristine cry, whimper or shriek? Did my flesh tear or rip, or did it do both? Cherry-picked, the words were a sponge. They soaked me up and wrung me out until all I could do was stare into space. My first draft, although accurate, was bereft of feelings and senses. Detailed, I had written about what my attackers were wearing, when they smoked and what they did. Over the months, I revisited every sentence, writing not only what I saw, but also what I heard, smelled, tasted and touched. I did not have to think about the plethora of emotions I experienced during the attack, because by connecting each sentence with my senses, it just happened; terror, debilitating uncertainty, disbelief, shock, and the waves of false hope, bordering on ecstasy, that they were going to let us go.

It wasn't just the attack, but the implications of it. The loss of a friend, health, independence, income; it felt like I was a grain of sand tossed around in a tornado. My world had spun out of control. I was angry because I was frightened. I was frightened because I was angry. Identifying the two helped me manage some of the PTSD, and understand the fallout on others. The world was a hostile place. I hardly left the house. Ragged, there was barely anything left in me to face the daily scuffles in Israeli life, challenges I had once enjoyed. Standing in line or sitting in traffic now had the effect of what I can only describe as a "brain freeze." The noise, the crowds, the aggressive banter, even the thought of being in these situations, sent me back into my room behind lock and key, where I would lie down and think of nothing, so stressed I couldn't think at all. Don't travel in rush hour, suggested Dr. Rozenberg. Pre-check the traffic, bring ear plugs, tell yourself you'll be home before long – and always remember, if you get in a situation and you really can't cope, just walk away.

Evaluating the oncoming stress, minimizing it, and keeping open the glorious option of walking away, if needed, were helpful. So was the sleep issue – or lack of it. Insomnia was chronic. I was dizzy and nauseous with exhaustion. There were no nightmares, just the reality. I slept no longer than a couple of hours at a time, becoming ever fearful I was tilting towards insanity.

A reframing of time helped. Rather than think of night and day, I learned to see time as a 24-hour chunk. It was somewhat liberating. The assumption that when it was dark I was meant to be sleeping, disappeared. The rule that people sleep when it's night and function when it's day no longer applied to me. I could doze anywhere at any time. And that was more than OK; the reframing of "shoulds" and "should nots" kept madness at bay.

And so I had learned to cope as best as I could with crowds, noise, insomnia and even trees. But to put myself in the vicinity of where my friend was murdered seemed premature. You will never feel it will be the right moment, Dr. Rozenberg told me on the phone. Her words echoed those of The Colonel, that night in hospital, when he handed me the phone to speak to Kristine's father.

"But it wasn't a dream. It was a place."

—Dorothy

CHAPTER 24

It is eight o'clock in the morning on the third day of Passover. Except for the skies, which are deep blue with little puffy clouds, the colors of spring are more pastel than those of autumn and fainter in the early morning. There is no hum of traffic coming from the Beit Shemesh road as there was that day. Traffic will start in an hour or so, when Israeli holidaymakers crowd to Horvat Hanut.

I head towards the place where my life changed, my skin wrinkled, my hair turned gray overnight, and ever since, bones that I never knew I had have never stopped aching. My destination is not so much a place as a space in time in which, after thirty minutes of madness, came the premature end of my life as I knew it, and the end of the life of a forty-four-year-old innocent Christian woman.

Pine cones are scattered on the ground. I recall how I picked up a couple and hurled them up ahead, watching how Peanut dashed out from a bush and jumped on my legs with her tongue lolling like some crazed beast.

With slackened steps and heart in mouth, I walk with Gidi Bashan, the forest ranger, whose tree trunk legs take strides three times the size of my own. There is no going back. Even though I am on flat ground, it feels as if I am walking uphill.

223

Gidi really is as huge as I recalled him to be when he came to the hospital that night. He puts his arm around me. My head doesn't even reach his chest. He squeezes my shoulder and tells me I'm a hero, and that like many people, including the doctors, he wasn't sure I would survive the night.

He went back that night to search for Kristine's body after he visited me in the hospital. Unknowingly, he stood only ten feet away from where she lay. But it was dark. Her body was hidden. It was not found until six o'clock the next morning, at the first appearance of light. There were over four hundred soldiers, volunteers and police all looking for Kristine. Everyone came to help. Absolutely everyone.

We reach the clearing sealed off by a single wire fence. Over the last year and a half, the saplings have been planted and have grown to young olive trees. Unlike Kristine, they have been nourished with life. Who would have known that the four freshly dug holes that looked like little graves were to be a foreshadowing of what was to come, and that within thirty minutes of her touching the russet earth, she would be lying on it, dead.

We continue until we reach the crossroads that lead down to the Roman steps. Gidi eyes the steep incline to the right and asks me if I am ready. We head up the hill through the thicket. The foliage is dense and more buoyant than it was that December day. There are no leaves on the ground and no thorns under my feet. The spring soil is soft and refreshed by the dew that has not long dried up.

At the brow of the hill, just as it did then, the Zanoah Brook looms below. Its once-famished jaws no longer gape in hungry expectation, hoping to swallow me as I plunge to my death. Content in its fertility from the winter rains, the sleepy valley yawns.

The Judaean Mountains bulge, not in a boastful show of strength protecting Jerusalem; this morning they swell with the blood of Kristine Luken. When I told her that day that our Patriarchs had walked those very hills, I remember her look of longing. She stared at them, or rather into them, her gaze unfocused, not moving her head even an inch. It was too dangerous to go there, I said. Only then did she look down. Grazing the ground with the tip of her shoe, she drew little lines in the dust. She did it again when I told her that King David's first capital was "out of bounds" and the birthplace of her Lord was now a Muslim town. Gracious as always, she smiled, her lips-only smile, not of disappointment but the one that she used if she thought someone felt bad. We will Google it when we get back, I told her.

That flat rock, I tell Gidi, that was our bench, the one on which we sat, giggling and spitting seeds into the breeze. It was our table, where Kristine tasted food for the very last time.

Sixty feet down the hill are the bushes where they hid. From there they performed their first act of evil. From there they asked for water in Hebrew, to find out if we were Jewish. From the moment they spoke, my heart sped up. Then it broke, shattered into pieces and hardened. It has never become whole again.

We walk east, down through the thicket, no more than thirty paces.

Everything, from the stone table to the spot where they jumped on us and held us at knifepoint to the arena of death occupied a smaller space than I had imagined.

Gidi takes my backpack and walks towards the shade of a tree. With drooping shoulders, the ranger stands in its shade, drawing deep breaths. I eye the lone carob tree with its rubbery leaves. Sixteen months ago, a murderer scratched his back against the trunk with a machete in one hand and a cigarette in the other.

We continue to follow the few steps they took us, gagged, bound and barefoot, to the top of the hill, our place of execution. Cypress trees, on guard, stand upright and rigid holding their branches tight to their trunks, refusing to bear witness to what was.

Gidi looks up and down, left and right, turns full circle, and then tells me I have nothing to worry about. I should take my time, he says. His massive hand grips the pistol strapped to his waist. He faces away from me to give me my privacy.

I look down. With my eyes, I follow a line of tiny green shoots that, like informants, poke through the dirt pointing to the spot where her blood was spilled. There is no monument or stone to mark the place. There is only a sprinkling of flowers. Pink flax flowers that were then hidden as seeds in the earth, but now, blushing with shame, tilt their heads. Desolate and utterly wretched, the little rosy facade marks the place where men danced with evil and stole the life of Kristine Luken.

Right here, where the pink flax flowers testify to spring, is where I first knew she was dead. Twelve hours later, I heard it on the lips of a friend. Throughout that day, others whispered it too. All spoke of that which should never be spoken, their voices hushed and shaky.

In this place was half an hour of powerlessness. Here, the human right to self-dignity, the right to carry out even the most basic of impulses, was stolen by the dread of what someone else set out to do to me.

The warm sun shines on my brow. I recall how I was hot then, yet it was dangerous to remove my fleece for fear that he might kill me for making a move. Begging for a sip of water to alleviate my thirst was a life-threatening request. Neither of us was entitled to speak without being spoken to or to express an opinion or have the right to be heard. We did not have the luxury of planning what to do next, let alone think about tomorrow. Neither of us had a say in whether we lived or died. We were not even given the time to prepare for our deaths.

Right here, without trial, she was pronounced guilty of the crime of "being a Jew." Right here she was murdered, in a secret place in a forest in Israel where the only witnesses to her death were me, her executioners, and a part-Jack Russell.

Kristine should have lived until she was ninety and then died in a soft bed under pink cotton sheets surrounded by her loved ones. She should have simply passed away, but she didn't. Slaughtered by a couple of savages, she was cheated of life and a natural demise.

Her death was not beautiful or peaceful. It was premature, unwanted, untamed, brutal, vicious, lonely and agonizing. It was a death where she was dispossessed of the right to say a final goodbye and prepare herself for the world to come. It was not the end of her life, but the theft of it. The blows smashed her bones, slashed her flesh, and their butcher's knife cut away her future.

If there is such a state of mind before death called "being at peace," then for me it was not so. My life never flashed before me, no angel reached down from Heaven to reassure me. Not one cell in me wanted to die or to go to another world. I can only imagine by the way she begged for her life, death did not do that for Kristine either.

But that, I will never know.

Putting my hands behind my back, I place one wrist over the other and pretend they are tied. Unhindered by the laces that once cut my skin, blood pumps palpably through my wrists. Then I kneel on that spot of execution.

Through the corner of my eye, the sun shines through the trees, soaking the earth with a pale and unapologetic light. That sun that I once thought I was seeing for the very last time has continued to rise and set.

I wait for the flash of steel. I wait to feel again that I am falling over a cliff. I wait to feel that I am swirling like the water in a bathtub, gathering velocity and being sucked into the unknown. I wait to be drained. I wait to be emptied. I wait to feel too scared to be frightened. And I wait for the holy creed of the *Shahada.*

It never comes.

"Shema Yisrael," I whisper. "Shema Yisrael," I say again, just because I can. I utter the *Kaddish,* the Jewish Mourner's Prayer, where death is not mentioned and God's name is praised. On my knees, under the April skies, I honor Israel's God in memory of a Christian woman.

Yitgadal v'yitkadash sh'mei raba. Glorified and sanctified be God's name.

And with a shudder, I recall that if it was not for *Kaddish,* Kristine Luken would not be dead, for she would not have come to Israel. It was deep in a Polish forest like this that I had first noticed her. She was leaning against the monument in the Sobibor death camp, where the Nazis murdered Jews. The monument was a red stone sculpture of a woman weeping and clutching her child. When I asked Kristine what she was doing, she told me she was reciting *Kaddish.* A Christian woman, stumbling through the Aramaic prayer in a place where thousands of Jews were murdered in the Holocaust, moved me profoundly. That's why I invited her to Israel, so she could meet the people she loved. Never did I imagine that I would be reciting *Kaddish* for her.

Gidi and I trace my walk of death back to the picnic table. The thicket is a tangled mass, almost impenetrable. He says it is hard to understand how even an able-bodied person could walk through it for over a mile without falling, let alone doing so after being stabbed and beaten, while gagged, bound, barefoot and uphill.

With my shoes on, the ground is acquiescent now, unable to claw my ankles or tear into the soles of my feet. The crickets chirp, the flies buzz and the birds warble without a care in the world. Holly oaks and top-heavy carobs mingle with grouchy olives, whose branches once clawed my clothes.

When I was dying, the tree trunks looked like the contorted faces of my grieving loved ones. Then, even the knots on the trunks were like eyes, swollen with sadness. Now they are absent of anguish. They are nothing but disinterested trees. The olive, a symbol of peace, looks helpless and feeble. The carob, a symbol of justice, stands aloof and uncaring, that those who didn't even know her name, found it right to take her life.

We arrive back on the National Trail. It is marked by fine sand. Now, like then, I hum "Somewhere Over the Rainbow," thinking of its lilting melody and tender chords. Murder was the music of that day. Murder was the chord that ended her life. Kristine was an unfinished symphony that inharmoniously stopped.

If only I had known that everything she did that day, from wrapping up pottery to writing in her notebook, would be for the last time. She packed her bag in the morning, unwittingly preparing for her death. If only I would have known, I would have cherished the present. If only I had not let go of those granules that made up her life.

We reach the picnic area. I sit down on a bench. Any moment now, I feel Kristine will peek out from behind a tree and tell me it was all a dream. But if she did, I would not believe that either. God knows, I want to feel her death, to breathe it and to weep at what man has done.

But I can't.

It will never be really believable. There was too much life in her childlike expression with her expectant green eyes brimming with wonder to believe that she is dead.

It feels like a dream.

But it wasn't a dream. It was a place.

"Now I know I've got a heart, 'cause it's breaking."

—Tin Man

CHAPTER 25

The second part of this spring Passover morning is for me to guide, or offer some sort of semblance of what could pass as "guiding," to groups of hikers. Talk about freedom, it's Passover, it's the Feast of Liberation, talk about all that, is what Ruti from the Tour Guide Association told me on the phone.

Under the puffy clouds, a group of about twenty children in blue shorts and oversized caps pulled over their ears play in the ruins of Horvat Hanut. The kids buzz with excitement. Their gleeful voices ring out like happy little flutes.

A girl of seven or eight tackles the ancient walls surrounding the mosaic. Defiant, enthusiastic, unstoppable and purposeful, she tosses her bag to the ground, stretches up her arms, grabs the stones and follows through with her legs until she is almost horizontal. Looking back over her shoulder at the three-foot drop below, she tells a chubby little boy standing nearby to come and see. The boy sweeps his bangs out of his eyes and looks up at the soles of her feet. She hangs from the wall and giggles. It is as if she is packing all of the joys of her life into this moment.

A woman with hair pulled back with a bright pink headband tells the girl to climb down. But the child is too wired. She is filled with excitement and unable to hear the shoulds and should nots. Life is clearly too thrilling. She has discovered a new world, an old world, a world of ancient stones.

Nothing is as good as hanging off this wall. No way will she come down, at least not for now.

Fathers carrying picnic baskets and mothers with pink-cheeked babies strapped to their backs mill around the far end of the mosaic, the same mosaic where Kristine brushed away the sand from the ancient inscription and remarked, "broken yet beautiful, it is an image of life itself." In the corner are still the same tatty old brushes, left by the Jewish National Fund. They have stood there for a year and a half, apathetic to what took place just a mile away.

One boy with thick round glasses and jug ears digs in the sand with his heels and marks out a line. This is his territory. This is where he is going to sweep away the sand and discover the mosaic. Two other boys tug at a broom, arguing who should use it first. Other children have no time for the brushes or brooms. Just as Kristine did, a little girl falls to her knees and scoops up the sand to let it run through her fingers.

The teacher calls for the children to gather around. Racing and squealing, they beeline towards her. When the teacher does a head count, every time she touches one of them on the head, they giggle. She puts her finger to her lip to signal them to stop fidgeting.

No, Liat, you cannot talk, not even quietly. No, Arik, not even for a few minutes. Sima, you have to settle down. Yes, Noam, that's right. The tour guide is going to talk to us.

The teacher comes over and introduces herself to me as Ilana. She tells me the children are special-needs kids. Do I know that, as part of their English lessons, they wrote letters to Kristine's parents. The Lukens were so touched they reciprocated and sent English textbooks for the school.

Ilana takes my arm. "They all come from broken homes," she says. "They are intensely aware of their own frustrations and limitations, but because of that, they are expressive, considerate and acutely able to identify with people in pain."

Arm in arm, she leads me to the children. Wide-eyed, the kids stare. They are fascinated, struck with awe, as if I am the first human being they have ever seen. A little girl with pigtails tugs at her teacher's sleeve. She coyly reminds the teacher that they have drawn me some pictures and put them in an album.

Ilana hands me a big white book. On the cover, written in blue, is: *To dear Kay Wilson, with love and admiration.* A crayoned rainbow arches over the writing.

A boy with thick glasses elbows his way to the front of the group. His voice is rushed, excited.

"Can I show Kay my picture please, teacher?" He shifts impatiently from one foot to the other.

"Yes, of course you can, Daniel," says Ilana. "Everyone is going to have their turn." The child grabs the book from my hands. With a furrowed brow, he thumbs quickly through the pages until he comes to a drawing of a muscled man with a black Mohican strip of hair running across the top of his scalp. The character has long eyelashes and glasses.

"Look!" he says. "'Shema Yisrael' is tattooed on your forehead."

Rather disconcertingly, the brawny figure has crimson lipstick and "Kay" slapped across its six-pack.

"That's you," he says, bright-eyed, clearly thrilled at the resemblance. "I drew you beating the terrorists." Wearing oversized army boots, "I" am standing on two bearded men who are lying on the ground. Above them are a couple of speech bubbles with the words "Help us!" and "Save us!"

The boy points to scores of gray lines sticking out of the men, which give them a somewhat hedgehog appearance. Those gray lines are what my penknife did. Apparently.

A girl with pigtails tugs the album out of his hands. "Look at mine," she says. "I wrote in English."

She flips through the pages until she arrives at a picture of seven yellow-faced angels standing on top of an Israeli Egged bus. Like an airplane after take-off, the bus cuts through blue skies and cotton clouds towards a line of fiery orange at the top of the page. A sticker of an American flag is on the end of what looks like a rope tied to the exhaust. There is only one passenger, a pencil-stick girl with green saucer eyes sitting in one of the windows. Along the side of the bus, crayoned in wobbly English letters, is "Shalom Kristine."

A pale boy with freckles tells me his name is Arik. He starts to say something else, but stops. It causes a significant amount of nudging and whispering. Ilana puts her finger over her lips.

"Everyone will have their turn," she says. "Just be patient. What did we learn last week? Yes, that's right, Sima, we learned to listen to others."

When the children quieten down, Arik says that from me, he learned to play dead.

"Well, not really dead," he says, correcting himself. "Just sick."

He tells me how it came about. It was in math class. He hates math. He thought that if he lay there with his head on the desk playing dead, he could get out of it. He even smeared olive oil on his face to make it look like he had died from a fever, but the teacher didn't believe him.

All the kids laugh. It is a chorus of manic giggling, a symphony of life. The teachers commands them to settle down again. It's time to hear the tour guide. Spellbound, every eye is on me.

In a shaky voice, I tell them that once upon a time, I didn't think I would ever hear children giggling again.

Why that one comment made them do what they do, I don't know, but one girl grabs my ankle, another wraps her arms around my legs, while two little boys hug me around the waist. Then one or maybe it is two children grab my arms. When one child peels himself way, vacating a particular limb, another child takes his or her place. Every part of me is taken. Every part is hugged.

Over the squealing and giggling, Ilana raises her voice. Does it bother me? Not at all, I manage to tell her. The kids clamber not just for my attention, but over each other, eager to tell me their names and what they have learned. Gone is the look of idol worship. I am now their best friend.

The teacher finally calls for calm. It's Rina's turn to speak.

In between blowing bubbles, Rina tells me how she has enjoyed everything much more since hearing my story. I should know that she covers her fries with ketchup at least a hundred inches thick. Stretching out her arms to demonstrate the hundred inches, she accidentally slaps little Rachel on the chin. While Rachel pouts, Rina waits for her classmates to stop laughing, using the time to practice her bubbles.

"What I wanted to say," she says rolling her eyes, "is that it was the most fabulous meal in the whole, wide world."

A little girl called Betty pokes Rina's shoulder in a "so there" sort of prod.

"Everyone adds ketchup," she says defiantly. "Not just you." She added mayonnaise, mustard *and* ice cream on hers, not just ketchup. Why ice cream, asks the teacher. Rina says it's because we won't live forever and ever and ever and ever and ever, and we should enjoy every moment.

Over the wane of gleeful applause, a plump little fellow with an airy voice tells me his name is Boaz. I recognize him as the boy who earlier was watching the girl clamber the wall. He pivots on his heels and stares at his soccer boots. His bangs droop over his eyes. These are his magic boots, he tells me. Only last week, it was with these very boots that he scored his first ever goal. He lifts up a chunky leg and hops clumsily in a circle to show me the shoe that helped him achieve the impossible.

"Kay, you didn't give up," he says, breathless. "So I didn't either. I'm a champion. I scored a goal."

This warrants gleeful applause.

Aside from the children, there are about forty adults who have gathered just outside the mosaic of Horvat Hanut. Edna Feinstein, the bubbly lady with a clipboard and the organizer of the event, tells them to get as close as they can. It is time to start. She explains how the event will take place. Along the Caesar's Path there will be tour guides stationed every third of a mile. Each guide will tell them a bit about the place. It is important to keep to time so there won't be a bottleneck of hikers.

She turns to me. "Are you ready to start, Kay?"

I unravel the piece of paper upon which is my ten-line speech. Against all the etiquette of the profession, I wrote down what I wanted to say. For weeks, I have deliberated over words and punctuation, culminating in a talk that will be no more than a minute long. It is a short speech that I have, by now, read many times, at night, first thing in the morning, and throughout the day.

Speaking in front of a crowd is something that guides thrive on. Yet now, under the Passover skies of Horvat Hanut, my stomach tosses and turns. Although it is only ten o'clock on a spring morning, I am sweating as if it is a midsummer afternoon.

The forest falls silent. Nothing moves except my hands. For want of trembling, I can't even hold the paper still. When I try to speak, the lump in my throat keeps any words from coming out. I can only look down. The mosaic resembles my life; broken, never to be whole again.

And then, I feel warm chubby fingers groping for my own. I look and see they belong to Boaz, the boy who scored a goal. In his other hand, he holds up his soccer boots.

"I want you to have my magic shoes," he says. "Because the bad men stole yours."

He drops his soccer boots, wraps his arms around me and stretches his neck back to look up at me. I push his bangs out of his eyes. Brimming with injustice, they also shine with kindness. For a fleeting moment, it is like looking into the face of God.

I turn my head and look down at the mosaic. It is a haze of chestnut, claret and bronze. For the first time since the murder of Kristine Luken, tears are in my eyes. Unstoppable, they run down my face and fall onto the broken mosaic.

The Rage Less Traveled

Epilogue

Under Palestinian Authority law, Kifah Ghanimat, Ayad Fatafta and thousands of other incarcerated terrorists receive financial rewards, in the form of monthly salaries, from the Palestinian Authority.

Since their arrest on December 20, 2010, my assailants have received more than $70,000 each. Even as this book goes to press, the money is still pouring in. These salaries will soon be raised. They will each receive $3,410 per month for the rest of their lives. These financial rewards come from monies donated by foreign governments – including the government of the United Kingdom, of which I am a citizen.

For years, I have tried to put a stop to this outrage. I have sent a letter to every single member of the British Parliament. Only six bothered to acknowledge they had received it. I have also appealed to the British media. Despite being a British citizen, the BBC, Sky News, LBC and other mainstream British television and radio stations have consistently ignored my requests for an interview. The most recent refusal was from the BBC in March 2019.

ABOUT THE AUTHOR

Kay Wilson is a tour guide, jazz pianist, cartoonist and motivational speaker. Since 2014, she has addressed a variety of audiences all over the world, speaking both of her ordeal and the survival skills she has employed to combat PTSD. She has done a TED talk, delivered a speech to the United Nations, and been interviewed for radio and television inside and outside of Israel. In her role as a representative of Palestinian Media Watch, she lobbies Western governments to end the foreign aid that rewards her would-be murderers with monthly salaries.

Together with a Muslim friend, Wilson has created the "Yellow Brick Road", an educational project that teaches children in a Palestinian refugee camp emotional intelligence, empathy and courage, with the goal of empowering them to stand up to adults who try to groom them and send them to their deaths.

Wilson, whose actions led to the capture of her assailants, has been recognized by the Israeli Police and the Israeli Security Agency for her courage. The attack was the subject of an acclaimed Israeli documentary, "Black Forest," broadcast in 2018.